GERMANY AND ENGLAND

GERMANY AND ENGLAND

By J. A. CRAMB, M.A.

LATE PROFESSOR OF MODERN HISTORY, QUEEN'S COLLEGE, LONDON

WITH A PREFACE TO THE AMERICAN EDITION BY

MOREBY ACKLOM

NEW YORK

E. P. DUTTON & CO., Publishers

1914

The Knickerbocker Press, New York

PREFACE TO THE AMERICAN EDITION

MORE and more clearly as the days pass, the European war stands out as a supreme conflict between England and Germany.

The nations may quarrel about the apportionment of the blame for the opening of the struggle; but Belgium's neutrality, Russia's mobilization, Servia's self-respect—these were merely sparks that led to the explosion. The powder to which these sparks set fire had been heaped up long since and added to every year.

To America, English in speech and origin, and of late increasingly German in intellectual outlook, an understanding of the true causes of this colossal clash, an accurate comprehension of what Germany is fighting for, and what England is resisting, is of peculiar interest.

In this little book, Professor Cramb, one of the few Englishmen profoundly saturated with German literature, German history, and German thought, shows how far back in history the motive of this conflict lies and why England and Germany, kindred people, both dowered with the spirit of empire, proud of the glorious past, are standing face to face, each in the other's way—and one of them *bound* to be humbled.

Since 1870, or from an even earlier date, the
German mind has been dominated by the ideas of
Treitschke, the leader of the Prussian school of
history and philosophy, which includes Droysen,
Haüsser and Sybel, Pertz and Delbrück. The
greatness of Prussia, the fated world-mission of
Germany under the supremacy of Prussia, is the
inspiration of all these men. In their eyes there
is only one obstacle to Germany's triumph, the
British Empire. The predominance of Britain
in world-politics is an insult, the mere existence
of the British Empire is an affront to them.
Treitschke attributes England's success to German
preoccupation with higher and more spiritual
ends; he looks on British colonial possessions as the
result of ingenious theft, treachery, and underhand
commercialism. Thus, to the German of to-day
the British Empire and the world-trade which
goes with it seem something of which his own
nation has been unjustly deprived, and of which
in the future his sword is to inevitably secure him
the rightful possession. Hence the "Weltmacht
oder Niedergang" battle-cry of Von Bernhardi
and the militarists.

On the other hand, Britain having through five
centuries fought incessantly for her Empire, and
having sacrificed incalculable treasure and innumerable lives to this magnificent monument of
her greatness, has now arrived at a point where she
wishes to consider the scramble for territory and

the changing of boundaries as closed. She has entered upon the period of conservation; her will is for peace and security just as the German will is for war and acquisition.

Professor Cramb, writing fifteen months before the war broke out, foresaw with the infallible eye of a master critic the symptoms of a gigantic conflict, as inevitable as the next sunrise, but which to England and her politicians was absolutely invisible and unthinkable.

Animated by the most profound admiration for the heroic spirit of Germany, for its splendid traditions, for its world-circling ambition, he, in this book, warns his own countrymen of the German state of mind. Never has an Englishman before so entered into the German point of view, never has the German passion for empire been so sympathetically and so powerfully explained. Professor Cramb finds much to praise in the war-spirit; he looks on it as something which, like religion, is super-rational, and therefore not to be criticized by the standards of commerce and every-day life.

The book is stimulating, suggestive, and nobly phrased. It will do more to put squarely before Americans the conflicting ideals at issue in the present war than all the writings of all the prolific newspaper critics.

It will also serve to open the eyes of the well-meaning pacificists, who anticipate that at the first considerable reverse on either side, the contestants will naturally be willing to entertain offers of friendly mediation from the United States, to the fact that this is no mere match-contest for "points," but a grim, life-and-death grapple of two eternally opposite principles, one of which *must* be overcome before any peace worthy the name can come to Europe.

Incidentally, it contains a warning for America which it would be a national blunder not to heed.

Germany and England was put together from the last course of lectures which Professor Cramb delivered; and his sudden death, about this time last year, prevented him from working out the concluding part of his subject as fully as he had intended.

The reader may not agree with all the ethical estimates of the author; but, even so, he can have no doubt that here is a very remarkable book indeed, full of fire, of insight, and of inspiration, a noteworthy herald of the terrific tempest which has since broken loose upon the world, even as the author predicted.

MOREBY ACKLOM.

New York, September 30, 1914.

CONTENTS

LECTURE III

TREITSCHKE AND YOUNG GERMANY

LECTURE IV

PAST AND FUTURE

GERMANY AND ENGLAND

LECTURE I

THE PROBLEM

I

THE purpose of these lectures demands perhaps at the outset some explanation. First of all, I disclaim any intention to provoke or foster hostile feeling between Englishmen and Germans. My aim, rather, is to contribute, as far as one can by encouragement and exhortation, to a mutual understanding between those of the two countries whom my words may reach. But the forces which determine the actions of empires and great nations are deep hidden and not easily affected by words or even by feelings of hostility or friendship. They lie beyond the wishes or intentions of the individuals composing those nations. They may even be contrary to those wishes and those intentions. Individual friendship or hate has a very fugitive and uncertain influence on war and peace; and the good or evil will, even of great numbers of private persons, has little effect on the ultimate motives that control the actions of States. It may be questioned whether in the twentieth century any *plébiscite* would ever be in favour of war. At the time of the Fashoda incident there were probably in France as many individual Frenchmen who entertained kindly feelings towards individual Englishmen as there are private persons entertaining such feelings to-day under the Entente Cordiale; and they had probably just as much influence on the reciprocal relations of the two governments. The history of the Republics of Hellas and of Italy is but a large comment on this theme. You may study its amplification in the two greatest philosophic historians of all time—Thucydides and Machiavelli. Napoleon understood this. "Politics is Destiny," he said on one occasion. "La politique, c'est la fatalité."

What then is my purpose? I answer in the words of a German historian, "To see things as in very deed they are." The prayer of Ajax in the dire extremity of the Greeks at Troy was for light that he might see his enemy's face. It is a noble prayer. What other prayer should be England's now?

The object, therefore, which I have immediately in view is to stress the value, if not the necessity, to Englishmen of a deeper understanding of

Germany, a deeper understanding of that great nation's political temper, its history, the motives of the actors who, in the past, have seemed to control that history; the development of its institutions and its laws, its poetry and its literature— ever the highest instructors in the aspirations of a race[1]; its present dreams and their relations to its past disillusionments or defeats. For in the history of nations there is a Fate, an inexorable *nexus* of things, which constantly arrests and constantly eludes our scrutiny, making the sequence of events in the history of such a people now seem inevitable as some dark and purposeful drama, now controlled by laws more akin to Nature and the elements than to the motives of human action.

Whether we regard Germany as a friend or as a foe, the aims and ideals of that nation, some ephemeral, some so deeply rooted in the past that they are beyond the power of the present to modify, are the aims and ideals which must singularly affect England in the present and are likely to con-

---

[1] There is no such stainless mirror of a nation's soul as German literature. In every age it is racy of German earth, going the round of its rivers and mountains and valleys. In the thirteenth century it is in Thuringia, the feudal castles; in the sixteenth, Saxony gives its tone to Reformation literature and hymns; the varied art of Silesia dominates the seventeenth, as that of Suabia the eighteenth century. Romanticism has its home in Berlin; the fatalism of Vienna and Munich succeeds "Young Germany"; and in the twentieth century Berlin again leads in this, one of the greatest of world-literatures.

tinue to effect England, beyond those of any other nation, for several generations to come.

If Germany is our enemy of enemies, if the twentieth century is to witness such a conflict for empire as that of England against France in the eighteenth century, or against Spain in the sixteenth, what is more imperative than that we should understand the spiritual as well as the material resources of that enemy, than that we should seek to discover the hidden foundations of its strength and probe the most secret motives of its actions, the characterizing traits of its policy, the deep convictions which mould the history of the nation? For with nations as with individuals, it is character that counts; he that wills greatly, conquers greatly.

If, on the other hand, Germany is to be England's friend, perhaps even her ally, if blood indeed be thicker than water, then perfect mutual understanding, the earnest scrutiny of our separate aspirations as they emerge from our separate pasts, can only strengthen that friendship and render that alliance more enduring. For there is no surer basis of friendship, whether between individuals or nations, than the sympathy that is born of knowledge and the knowledge that, in turn, is produced by sympathy.

Yet how far from that knowledge and how indifferent to its attainment are the majority of Englishmen in these times! Germany has one of the greatest and most profound schools of poetry —yet how many Englishmen have the secret of its high places or access to its templed wonders? Since the decline of Alexandria there has been no such group of daring thinkers as those of Germany in the later eighteenth and early nineteenth centuries; yet to most English men and women the "Critique of Pure Reason" and the larger version of Hegel's "Logic" are sealed as the "Enneads" of Plotinus.

Merely as an unexampled opportunity for the study of the soul of a people why should England neglect this literature? Why in 1913 should the following characteristic incident be even possible? A few weeks ago the head master of one of our public schools exhumed a letter of the late Mr. Gladstone, in which that eminent politician cast a slur upon the whole of German literature, denouncing the author of "Faust" and of "Iphigenie" as an immoral writer in whose works we find virtue banished and self-indulgence reigning. Yet Goethe is, perhaps, the most serene artist in words since Sophocles, and amongst the children of men not one has striven with a loftier purpose to divine, even though darkly, the bond of the Many and the One, and thus to justify the ways of God to man and of man to God. That in the welter of literary opinions, published and unpublished, of the late Mr. Gladstone, such a verdict on Goethe and on German literature should exist is not

astonishing. The astonishlng thing is that in the
second decade of the twentieth century an Englishman should have been found who, having exhumed
such a verdict, did not from very shame instantly
cover it again in complete oblivion. Instead of
this, he incontinently published it in the "Times,"
not once only, but in two different issues. The
publication of this letter is discreditable at once
to the critic, to the exhumer, to the press and to
the nation.

I have neither the wish nor the hope that every
Englishman should become a master of the German language and a learned student of the philosophy or the poetry of Germany, its history or its
politics. My ambition is more modest. It is
the hope that during the next few decades there
may gradually arise here in England a wall, as
it were, of cultured opinion, which should make
the blunt enunciation of such judgments by a
prominent politician all but impossible by the
ridicule to which they would at once expose him,
and their ratification by the head master of one
of our public schools absolutely unthinkable.

I have no desire to labour the point, but it is
difficult to pass in silence some of the most glaring
instances of our indifference even at the universities to German history and therefore to German
politics. Not a page of Treitschke's greatest
work has been translated; yet his history of the
first stages of Prussia's wrestle for supremacy,

his literary essays and his lectures on political theory, excite a more ardent curiosity in modern Germany than the essays and the history of Macaulay did in mid-Victorian England. Giesebrecht's great history of the early Empire, with its vivid portraiture of the tragic figures of the Saxon and the Suabian lines, is still inaccessible to all but a small minority of Englishmen; and its companion work, a masterpiece at once in erudition and in thought, as well as one of the most alluring of books, the "Verfassungsgeschichte" of Georg Waitz—are there fifty Englishmen living who have turned its grave and weighty pages or even heard its name? It would be easy to multiply instances; for German scholarship has not left a single period in its annals unillumined by some work which is marked by distinction or power and yet remains untranslated into English.

Yet of Germany beyond most nations it holds good that he who would understand its present or its immediate future must be content patiently to search for the key to its hieroglyphics in the past; and, above all, he who would estimate at their true significance the regret for missed opportunities of empire and the hopes of redeeming those opportunities which flit before the imagination of thinkers like Treitschke, or soldiers like Bernhardi, must feel the spell which the shadowy grandeur of the lost empire of the Ottonides and the Hohenstaufen still exercises over the mind of every German not sunk in sloth or chained to self-interest.

And the average Englishman, thus denied by his ignorance of the language all access to this deeper knowledge—to what sources of information does he trust? We know them well. There is, for instance, the Radical member of Parliament who, liberated from the cares of State, spends three weeks in Berlin, consorts with members of the Reichstag, and finds each and all of them thoroughly well-disposed towards peace with all men and with England in particular. What scaremongers are these, he asks indignantly, who talk of German ambitions or a German invasion? Then there is the geographer and traveller who spends a somewhat longer period in the towns and villages of Brandenburg and West and East Prussia, and returns aghast at the intensity of hate which he found—at what he describes as "the all but insane desire for war with England" which animates every class of society. There is, again, the statistician who enumerates the mileage of German railways and German canals, of Berlin streets and Berlin drains; or, again, the English officer of a type not yet obsolete, who, preparing for the Intelligence Department of the War Office, spends three months in Germany and finds in it "a nation of damned professors."

Thus, seeking reality, we find only appearance, and, pursuing knowledge, we gain only opinions—δόξαι, in the strictest Greek sense of that term.

This, then, is my general purpose in these lectures—to consider the deep strivings of German history; to understand what are the forces which are shaping the present in Germany, forces which lie far deeper than such momentary ebullitions of goodwill as were expressed a short time ago by Admiral Tirpitz. These are but things of a day. It is in the past of Germany that we must seek the real springs of the future action of Germany, whether that future be against England or with England.

II

DURING the last few months there has been in the hands of a large number of Englishmen and of tens of thousands of Germans a very remarkable book—a book which has sprung from those deeper fountains of a nation's history to which I have referred. It is a book written in German by a distinguished cavalry soldier, General von Bernhardi, and it has for its title and subject matter "Germany and the Next War"—"Deutschland und der nächste Krieg"—a problematical war, observe. What is the character of this work?

One of many similar books which during the past ten or twelve years have been widely read in Germany, it has an extraordinary interest for us, and an interest of a many-sided kind. It is a

fair and a just book—according to the writer's
insight; soldier-like in its simplicity, soldier-like
in its misdirected literary admirations. It has a
distinct significance, not only because of its military criticism, but because of its knowledge of
German history and civilization; for General von
Bernhardi is something of a scholar as well as a
distinguished soldier.[1] Like many German officers, he has attempted to understand not only his
profession as a soldier but the "why" of that
profession; studying the history, the literature, the
politics, and even the philosophy of his nation,
seeking the answer to the question: What is
Germany?

And by "Germany" he understands the vital,
onward-striving force flowing in German blood
from an endless time down to the present, and from
the present flowing onwards into an endless future.
What, he asks, is the precise value, the precise
significance of that force in its present manifestation—"Germany"? And he has a perfectly
definite answer: It is strife; it is war. And the

---

[1] I have selected General von Bernhardi's works not because
of any peculiar or distinctive value in them, but because, of all
that mass of literature from Treitschke to Delbrück, Schmoller,
and Maurenbrecher, they are the sole exemplars in Englishmen's
hands. For the rest, "Deutschland und der nächste Krieg," like
Bernhardi's earlier writings, is characterized by a certain diffuse-
ness. He is a reader of Nietzsche, but his style shows not a trace
of that master's pointed and lucid manner. It has, however, the
merit of entire sincerity.

direction of that strife? It is the isolation of Russia by bribes; the destruction of the antagonistic force named France beyond the power of raising her head; and thereafter Germany will be face to face with the day of reckoning with England. "The Hour" to which German officers of a Chauvinist tendency drink, will then have struck.

In the history of nations we must count time by decades or even by centuries. Under changeful moods of furious declamatory anger, as in the crisis of the Boer War, and under the mood of momentary *rapprochement* of the present day in the crisis of the reawakening of the national spirit in France, this steady thought persists. That is one interest of the book. There is, again, the interest which centres in any attempt made by a German to explain to himself England and Germany in their relations to one another; and this is one of the underlying thoughts throughout the book.

Again, the book has the interest derived from the fact that it represents a very strong trend of German, and, above all, of Prussian opinion—that accumulating mass of determined anti-Englishism. It is useless to see in Bernhardi's book the expression of a morbid or heated Jingoism. It is no rhapsody on war. Bernhardi is not a man who takes any excessive pleasure in the contemplation of war; on the contrary! But he is a man who recognizes those darker, obscurer forces shaping

the destiny of nations. To him this war with
England is inevitable. And his book is sympto-
matic; that is to say, it represents the mood, the
conviction, the fervent faith, of thousands and
tens of thousands of Germans—Prussians, Saxons,
Suabians, Bavarians.

Its philosophy is derived from Nietzsche and
Treitschke. In its military character the book is,
like General von Bernhardi's other writings, emi-
nently up to date. But what marks out this work
from all others of the same kind, giving it something of the distinction of a really epoch-making
book, is that it represents a definite attempt made
by a German soldier to understand not merely
how Germany *could* make war upon England most
effectively, but why Germany *ought* to make war
upon England. It is in this respect that the book
focuses the thoughts of many German writers,
historians, thinkers, novelists, pamphleteers, who,
again and again, for quite the last forty years,
have bent their attention to this subject.

Is it possible to find any moral, any ethical
justification for a war upon England? The war
of 1870 with France was a war of great revenge, of
just revenge, and for one of the greatest of causes.
No war in history, perhaps, was ever more just
than the war which Bismarck and Moltke waged
against France. When she comes to this war upon
England, on the other hand, Germany is face to
face with the difficulty that here she has no such

motive of retributive justice or revenge. And therefore you find a tendency to shape the question thus: How do England and her Empire stand in the path of the deepest desires and ambitions, and perhaps, also, the highest and most sacred aspirations of Germany?

If we ask what those desires, ambitions, and aspirations are, the answer is this: Germany, not less than England, it is contended, is dowered with the genius for empire, that power in a race which, like genius in the artist, must express itself or destroy its possessor. An empire she once had, centuries before France and England fought. That empire is lost. But in the German race the instinct for empire is as ancient and as deeply rooted as it is in the English race; and in the Germany of the present time, above all, this instinct, by reason of the very strength of Germany within herself, her conscious and vital energy, her sense of deep and repressed forces, is not a mere cloud in the brain, but is almost an imperious necessity. This is the real driving-force in German politics, the essential thing.

Hence the further question which young Germany asks is the question which Treitschke asks: At what point in her history did Germany swerve from the path to empire? Can she again find that path, or is it irrecoverably lost? Germany, from her own inward resources, produces year by year greater surplus energy, mental and physical, than any other nation in the world; yet year by year, by emigration to America, to England, and to other lands, that surplus energy is lost to her. Year by year are we to look on in impotent anger or in apathy whilst the best and most enterprising of our citizens quit the Fatherland and, living under other governments, cease to be Germans, bequeath their worth, that is to say their valour, to those nations who may be ultimately Germany's deadliest enemies?

These are the problems which, at the present hour, press in upon the mind of every thinking German. They have been the study of serious historians like Oncken, Treitschke, Mommsen, Sybel, even of Droysen. They are the questions which find their answer in novelists, poets, publicists and politicians. Pamphleteers like Eisenhart and Bley here agree with men of academic rank like Schmoller and Maurenbrecher, Franke, and Müller.

And the answer now given to the further question, What stands in the way of those desires and aspirations? is: Germany has one enemy. One nation blocks the way. That nation is England.

Thirty years ago this answer was vague; but since that period it has steadily grown more distinct; and since 1898 and the formation of the Navy League, since the South African War and the extraordinary outburst of political and personal hatred against England at that time, it has grown still more precise.   Not Russia or Austria, unless secondarily, not France, unless incidentally, is Germany's enemy: the enemy of enemies is England.   She bars the way to the realization of all that is highest in German life.

The enemy having thus been ascertained, the question which every German has to face is: Why are we to submit to this?

It is true that amongst Germans of every rank and class there are men willing to acknowledge the part which England has played in the past, who are perfectly willing to admire our Shakespeare, our dramatists, some of our historians, and are even willing to extend a kind of tolerant contempt to some of our philosophers.   But there are Germans of another kind, men of the type of Eisenhart and Bley, and, above all, of the type of Treitschke, whose attitude towards England is totally different.   These men, as the justification for this war, this "nächste Krieg," point to the broad fact—broad enough, assuredly!—that the English race is the possessor, "by theft," as Treitschke described it, of one-fifth of the habitable globe.   And they ask: "By what right?   By the right first of craft, then of violence!"[1]   German indignation then takes the place of German analysis.   Cooped up between the North Sea and the Danube, the

[1] "In 1839, in the midst of a time of peace, the rock-nest of Aden, the key to the Red Sea, the Gibraltar of the East, was stolen."   (Treitschke's "Deutsche Geschichte,"vol. V., p. 63.)

Rhine and the plains of Poland, conscious of our strength, exerting an ever stronger pressure upon our frontiers—can we or ought we, it is asked, to acquiesce in England's possession of one-fifth of the globe? Ought a patriotic German to submit to seeing his nation depleted year by year? Can he, on those conditions, retain his manhood or be true to the religion of valour, the birthright of the Teutonic kindred? It is very well for England to protest that she has no aggressive designs against Germany; England's mere existence as an empire is a continuous aggression. So long as England, the great robber-State, retains her booty, the spoils of a world, what right has she to expect peace from the nations? England possesses everything and can do nothing. Germany possesses nothing and could do everything. What edict then, human or divine, enjoins us to sit still? For what are England's title-deeds, and by what laws does she justify her possession? By the law of valour, indeed, but also by opportunity, treachery, and violence.[1]

[1] It is impossible in Germany to ignore the force of literary and academic ideas. Just such a series of irrelevant and inflammatory declamation, partly the work of the Tugendbund, partly the work of men like Arndt and even Stein, preceded the rising against Napoleon; and in a later decade just such a series preceded the war against Austria and the war against France. The causes of the wars of 1866 and 1870 can be so treated as to appear the work of professors and historians. What is Droysen's "History" but a pamphlet in six volumes in which Prussia stands

In the time of Roon and Moltke the attitude of Germans when the question of enmity to England was discussed was always, "Is it possible to land a German army upon English soil? And, once landed there, how is it possible to bring it safely back again with its plunder to the shores of the Elbe and the Rhine?" What was argued was a problem of abstract strategy, rather than of political or national aim.

A generation has passed. The heroes of the war of 1870 have one by one disappeared—Bismarck, Roon, Moltke, Manteuffel. That problem of strategy does still exist in Germany, but it occupies a much less prominent place than it occupied thirty or forty years ago. It seems to have solved itself during the last ten or fifteen years. It has become a secondary matter, and the quasi-historical form which the question of enmity to England now assumes in the minds of thousands of intellectual Germans is this: As the first great united action of the Germans as a people, when they became conscious of their power, was the overthrow of the Roman Empire, and ultimately, in Charlemagne and the Ottonides, the realization of the dream of Alaric—the transfiguration of the world, the subversion of Rome,

---

out as the model State? And the "French Revolution" of Sybel is a counterpart of the writings of Droysen and Treitschke in its arraignment of the French nation.

and the erection upon its ruins of a new State; so, in the twentieth century, now that Germany under the Hohenzollern has become conscious of her new life, shall her first great action be the overthrow of that empire most corresponding to the Roman Empire, which in the dawn of her history she overthrew? In German history the old Imperialism begins by the destruction of Rome. Will the new Imperialism begin by the destruction of England?

III

THE ethico-political or moral origins of the sentiment of antagonism between England and Germany are thus obvious enough—the confrontation of two States, each dowered with the genius for empire; the one, the elder, already sated with the experience and the glories of empire; the other, the younger, apparently exhaustless in resources and energy, baulked in mid-career by "fate and metaphysical aid," and now indignant.

This is the moral, the most profound source of antagonism; and its roots lie deep in European history—German historians as widely apart in mind as Hegel and Treitschke seeing the cause of Germany's frustrate destiny in her pursuit of ideal ends, of "the freedom of the spirit"; in her deep absorption in religion at the period when England, Holland, France, Spain, fired by com-

mercialism, played against each other for the
dominion of this planet. This is clear: this is the
ethical, the permanent and the real cause. It has
the characteristics of all true causes: universality
and necessity. And it is worth while pausing at
this point to ask the question: What is its historical
genesis?

The unity of modern Germany is the work of
Prussia and the great Hohenzollern dynasty.
What are the stages in the evolution of the relations between England and Prussia? There are
four distinct phases: the period of Frederick the
Great, the Napoleonic, the mid-nineteenth century
and the later nineteenth century.

The definite relations of England and Prussia
as State to State are synchronous with the history
of Prussia as a kingdom; and in the first decades
the terms are those of friendship. The son of the
Great Elector, Frederick I, as first King of Prussia,
sends his contingent to support Marlborough and
Eugène. During Frederick the Great's time, England's relations to Prussia, beginning in hostility,
owing to the sympathy of the English people
for Maria Theresa, and their enmity to France,
pass through a phase of variegated sullen friendship and alliance, and end again, at least on
Frederick's part, in clear burning hostility and
contempt when the government of Lord Bute
abandons Prussia. Minor German historians have
dwelt much on 1762 and the "betrayal" of

Frederick by the Cabinet of St. James's in the hour of his darkest fortunes.[1] Frederick, in his correspondence on the subject, does not spare the character of Lord Bute; but he is too profound an observer of the life of States, and too frequent a student of "Il Principe" and, above all, of "Gli-Discorsi," not to know that alliances between States are based on self-interest.

A generation passes. At the time of the Revolutionary and Napoleonic wars, England is for nearly eight years the enemy of Prussia, the enemy, that is to say, of Napoleon's ally, or Napoleon's tributary State. Then in 1813, 1814, and 1815, England stands side by side with Prussia, and this friendship is not interrupted during the Holy Alliance, though it is easy to trace distrust and misgiving in the attitude of actual Prussians or of "nationalized" Prussians, Prussians by sympathy like Niebuhr and Stein. These die. "They see," I have elsewhere said, "the world rushing upon ruin; they see the unchaining of anarchy. But what do they hope from England? England, faster than all the rest, is plunging down the steep."

With the Revolution of February, 1848, with 1870 and 1875, it is possible already to discern the

---

[1] The "Annual Register," which began in 1758, is, in its first numbers, full of proofs of the admiration felt by England for the King of Prussia. The Buckingham Correspondence indicates that Frederick's proud hostility was not to the nation, but to Bute.

rise of the present hostility.   And the underlying
cause, the *causa causans*?   It is interesting; it is
curious; it presents one of those movements, one
of those visible invisible "curves" traced in the
Unseen, which in history affect the imagination
like the great achievements in art.   The workshop
is flung open; we seem to witness the very operation of Fate; the Norns are weaving the destinies
of men.

This *causa causans* is not England.   England
is passive.   The active agent is Prussia.   Stage
by stage from the days of the Great Elector Prussia
has risen, guarding each advance with a Roman
precision and care.   Under her first two kings,
Frederick I and Frederick William I, as under
the Great Elector, Prussia is admirable in her
self-restraint.   Her aim is to secure the territory
extorted from the Swedes at Fehrbellin and to
organize the new kingdom.   She does not as yet
even come forward as Austria's antagonist,
despite ultra-Habsburg treachery, ultra-Habsburg
insolence.

Prussia strikes when her hour strikes, and in
1740, with the accession of Frederick the Great,
that hour does strike; and for the next twenty-
three years Prussia appears as the great rebel-
State, asserting herself triumphantly, measuring
herself in battle after battle against Austria and
Austria's allies.   All Europe cannot break her
spirit or the spirit of her king.

It is one of the lofty and exhilarating heroisms of world-history, this conflict of reality against empty formalism; of the substance of Frederick's military State against that phantom, the Army of the Empire; of right and strength against boastful weakness parading as power, unrighteous privilege decking itself with the sanctity of history and right.[1]

Nothing is more merciless than Frederick's mockery of that venerable myth, the Holy Roman Empire. We hear already Frosch's song in "Faust":

> "Das liebe, heil'ge, Röm'sche Reich
> Wie hält's nur noch zusammen?"

If the conflict at times is tragic, as in 1759 it becomes tragic, it is always heroic tragedy. Frederick's poetry before Rossbach moves us as the midnight talk of Achilles and Priam—the sorrow and the heroism in things:

> 'Pour moi, menacé du naufrage,
> Je dois, en affrontant l'orage,
> Penser, vivre et mourir en roi."

[1] "His statecraft bears on its face the stamp of his own kingly frankness. In the conflicts of States he had regard only for living things, for power skilfully utilized through rapid action. He gave truth once more a place of honour in German politics." (Treitschke's "Deutsche Geschichte," vol. I., pp. 49–50.)

And again we have at once to admire Prussia's irresistible and resolute advance and her strict restraint. Definitely she comes forward as Austria's rival; but the hour for Austria's overthrow has not yet come. Frederick's army and the *entrain* of success might have led, after 1763, into wars for world-empire which would have recalled those of Louis XIV and anticipated those of Napoleon. The king is not yet old—the age of Marlborough at Blenheim, of Cæsar at Munda. In Treitschke's theory, Frederick is conscious in himself of military genius like that of Alexander, yet is content with Prussia. Even when such men as Winterfelt or Dessau propose the Empire, he answers them: "No; it would be too awkward a burden."

Two generations pass. The War of Liberation follows, investing Prussia with a glory such as the war against Xerxes gave Athens. Blücher, Stein, Gneisenau, Scharnhorst, Arndt, Körner, Fichte, Kleist, Uhland, form a galaxy of heroism on which, between 1815 and 1848, the imagination of Young Germany broods not less ardently than, in an earlier generation, the contemporaries of Goethe and Herder had studied in Plutarch the heroic phantoms of Greece and of Rome. Then, when a century has passed since Frederick's wars, the task which, greatly daring, he declined, Prussia, greatly, wisely daring, now can undertake. The hour has once more struck. And at Sadowa and at Metz, Wörth and Sedan, she founds the new German nation and the new German empire.[1]

What is to be the next stage? Germany after 1870 finds a greater strength and a sense of more complicated and intricate unity than she ever possessed in the days of mediæval Imperialism; and in the House of Hohenzollern the new nation has found, in answer to all its aspirations, a dynasty not less heroic, not less great than the Ottonides or even the Hohenstaufen.

Now it is just at this moment in her history that Germany comes sharp up against England, as in the eighteenth century she comes up against Austria, and in the nineteenth against France. Yet in her past relations to England, Prussia, it may seem at first, can find no cause, personal and rancorous, such as animates her in 1760 or in 1870. From Austria and from France she had endured insult upon insult, measureless humiliations. But from England?

England's possessions, England's arrogance on the seas, her claim to world-wide empire—these, Germany answers, are to Germany an insult not less humiliating than any she has met with in her past. And what are these English pretensions? And upon what are they based? Not upon England's supremacy in character or intel-

---

[1] Bismarck now is *not* content with Prussia; he is for empire, though again temperate—"I wish to be an honest broker."

lect.   For what is the character of this race which thus possesses a fifth of the habitable globe and stands for ever in the path of Germany's course towards her "place in the sun," in the path of Germany's course towards empire?

It is from this first recrimination that, during the last three or four decades, largely under the influence of the Prussian School of History, there has been evolved a portrait of England as the great robber-State.   In one phase or another this conception is gradually permeating all classes, making itself apparent now in a character in fiction, now in a poem, now in a work of history or economics, now in the lecture-hall at Bonn or Heidelberg or Berlin, now in a political speech.

And the theme is precise.   England's supremacy is an unreality, her political power is as hollow as her moral virtues; the one an arrogance and pretence, the other hypocrisy.   She cannot long maintain that baseless supremacy.   On the sea she is rapidly being approached by other Powers; her resources, except by immigration, are almost stationary, and her very immigration debases still further her resources.   Her decline is certain.   There may be no war.   The display of power may be enough, and England after 1900, like Venice after 1500, will gradually atrophy, sunk in torpor.   An England insensibly weakened by brutalization within and the encroachments of an ever-increasing alien element, diseased or

criminal, and, by concession on concession without, sinking into a subject province though nomi-
nally free, whilst Canada, South Africa, Australia,
New Zealand, carves out each its own destiny—
such an England is easily conceived.

Who is to succeed her? It may not be Germany; some Power it must be. But if Germany
were to inherit the sceptre which is falling from
her nerveless hands . . . ?

And, having visualized this future, the German
imagination, in a tempest of envy or vehement
hate, becomes articulate and takes various shapes,
resulting in an almost complete arraignment of
the British Empire, of the English character, and
of all our institutions and all our efforts as an
empire-building race.

IV

First there is the general indictment of British
Imperialism as an influence upon humanity. You
acquired your empire, these critics say, by measureless treachery, violence, the perfidious foment-
ing of strife, and you have failed as an empire at
once in your colonies and in your dependencies.
Your colonies already shiver with impatience under
the last slight remnant of your yoke. The arrogance or the clumsiness of some beef-witted minister will alienate Canada or Australia exactly as
the clumsiness of the Graftons, the Norths, the

Grenvilles, between 1763 and 1775, alienated the New England States.

Then the German *Cultur-Imperialisten*, not un-affected probably by the study of Mommsen or of Curtius, certainly strongly influenced by the study of Dahn and Nietzsche, arraign the century and a half of our rule in India. "Your dominion," they say, "has been retrograde and obscurantist. India is not only the Italy of Asia; it is not only the land of romance, of art and beauty. It is in religion earth's central shrine. India *is* religion. Yet what consciousness of this have Englishmen ever exhibited? You came to India with an opium pipe in one hand and a Bible in the other. India, seeking dreams, accepted with the passion of de-spair the opium; it gave her dreams. Your Bible she rejected with measureless contempt, and she awoke from her opium sleep to fasten her eyes and her soul with new ardour, new adoration, on the great scriptures of her race. Yet the officers of your army and your civil administrators are in-capable of reading a page of those scriptures. Instead of seizing the opportunity of a new and great religious experiment, you, the conquerors—borrowers of your own religion—have come to the most original race of this planet and asked them to borrow from the borrowers!

"With what contempt for the conquerors must not the Brahmin, sunk in the studies of those vast and austere conceptions which by the vanished

stream of the Saraswati first allured the human
soul, rise at midnight from his studies and, as he
walks to and fro under the stars, console himself
for his lost nationality by pondering the problem,
poignant in its sarcasm as in its pathos: Which is
the greater humiliation to a race, to be indebted
to another for its government or to be indebted to
another for its religion? Germany, on the other
hand, is year by year preparing to make this great
religious experiment. The development of German
thought, from Kant to Fichte, from Hegel and
Schopenhauer to Lotze, Hartmann and Nietzsche,
strives to no other term.

"Thus in the spheres of religion and of thought
you have failed to impress your dominion upon the
Hindu imagination: the seed-fields of that failure
are rolling on to the harvest. The verses of one of
your own poets, pointless when applied to Rome
and Egypt, acquire a bitter meaning when applied
to England and India as but yesterday they were
applied by one of Ramakrishna's disciples educated
in England:

>"'The East bowed low before the blast
>In patient, deep disdain,
>She let the legions thunder past
>And plunged in thought again.'

"Nevertheless, though thus failing in religion,
you might have succeeded as Consular Rome succeeded in Hellas. Failing to impress your dominion on India by sovereignty of mind or by the

daring of speculative thought, you might still have impressed the imagination of the Hindu by your valour and by your organized strength in war. To the three hundred millions of Hindus you might have presented yourselves as a great Kshatriya race, a nation of warriors. Instead of this you attempt to hold India with almost fewer legions than Rome required to govern the original despicable race of Britannia. You invite hundreds of young Hindus of ancient lineage to your universities and to your schools. With what feelings must they read the tirades against a Nation in Arms, the litanies in praise of peace, which argue the slave and the coward at heart! Instead of a nation of Kshatriyas you appear as a nation of Vaisyas— a nation of shopkeepers indeed! You alone of the nations of Europe in the twentieth century still possess a mercenary army! Only at one period of your history, Treitschke affirms, did you ever possess a national army, and that was in the time of Cromwell.[1] When Englishmen ceased to be soldiers they forfeited their right to govern India in perpetuity.

"Thus in India you have failed conspicuously, ignobly and completely, because as a government and as a nation you have lost, if you ever possessed them, the three qualities revered by the Hindu race—creative genius in religion, the valour in arms of a military caste, and the pride of birth of

[1] Treitschke's "Politik," vol. II., p. 358.

the rajah. But chiefly you have failed because you
have ceased to be soldiers; because you dread war;
because you present to the whole world the spec-
tacle which the world has not seen since the fall of
the Byzantine Empire—a timorous, craven nation
trusting to its fleet.

"And as you have failed in India, so you will fail
in Egypt, which, next to India, is the most sacred
region on this earth. As yet you have succeeded
only in vulgarizing it. The Mamelukes spared the
majesty of the Pyramids. Napoleon, turning from
them, could make his great appeal, 'Soldiers, forty
centuries look down upon your actions!' But you
crept into possession of Egypt, by the weakness of
France, like a fox creeping into a farm-steading."

A different group of critics direct the indictment
against various aspects of our civic and national
life, against our morals, the administration of our
laws, our universities, and even against that palla-
dium, that happy *via media*, the Anglican Church.
It is affirmed with regard to the national religion of
England that that religion which we are proud of
naming "Catholic" nevertheless is the most provincial of all the creeds born of the Reformation.
Luther, Calvin, even Zwingli, can claim adherents
in other countries than those in which the faith of
each was founded. But Anglicanism—where are the
proselytes from other nations who have adopted
that as their life-giving hope? And its annals
since its institution are as barren or as provincial

as its doctrine and its ritual. What single name of European power in the eighteenth or nineteenth centuries has it produced? And at the present hour it has not a bishop whose name is known beyond the boundaries of his own diocese, or a single theologian who has any claim to the attention of mankind except such as is derived from his study of the German masters in his own science. And even in the sphere of theological criticism where is the English Reuss or Renan, where is the English Friedrich Strauss?

The criticism of our universities, rills from the German Parnassus, is so old and still so well justified that it would be tedious to repeat it. A new touch is contributed by Dr. Karl Bötticher, who tells us in effect: "You govern millions who read their sacred books in the Sanscrit and Arabic characters; but the fairest specimens of those types are still cast in German fonts. A German taught you the meaning of the religion of that province which you regard as the brightest jewel in the English crown; and to German scholarship you owe the initiatory impulse to study each of the four great world-religions of your empire—Mohammedanism, Zoroastrianism, Buddhism, and Brahminism." Or again, it is pointed out that Macaulay, our greatest national historian, makes mistakes in philosophy which no German *Fuchs* would commit.[1]

[1] "Macaulay exhibits a lack of philosophic culture that abso-

Contained also in this indictment is the charge against English law, arising out of the English Press criticisms of the German trials of English spies a short time ago. It is asserted that here too England is taking the downward course.

The critics pass on to consider other points of our life—our army, for instance, for which they have nothing but contempt. "You boast that the English flag is propped on the bones of the English dead; but from Blenheim to La Belle Alliance[1] German valour was prodigal of German blood in winning your victories. Gibraltar itself was captured for you by a foreign force led by a German prince; the right wing at Blenheim was scattered and the day lost when young Dessauer—not yet the old Dessauer—wrested victory from disaster;[2]

---

lutely amazes us Germans. He says things that with us no student would dare to say. . . . A comparison of Ranke with Macaulay brings out the contrast between German profundity and English superficiality." (Treitschke's "Politik," vol. II., p. 359.) Emerson's opinion, expressed in his "English Traits," is the same.

[1] "La Belle Alliance," "Schönbund," the designation for Napoleon's last battle consistently used by Prussian historians, *e.g.*, Häusser, Sybel, Droysen, Schlosser.

[2] [NOTE.—*This, of course, is an extreme instance of partial statement by such critics. At Blenheim the right wing (under Eugène) was never "scattered," though it was repulsed; it was not Dessau but Marlborough who changed his plan, concentrated on the French centre, and thus broke their line. At Gibraltar, the share of the fleet under Rooke, who first bombarded the town and then landed the capturing force, is ignored.*]

and yet once more, on the 18th of June, 1815, the advance of Blücher and his corps of Prussians saved your army from annihilation. And did not Professor Delbrück inform us during the Boer War that your soldiers on the march chained Boer women together in order to form a screen to protect themselves from the bullets of outraged husbands and fathers? And do we not know from discussions in our *Kriegsschule* that your soldiers have laid down their arms when every tenth man, and sometimes every fifteenth man, was wounded; whereas in 1870 our Germans stood unyielding even when every third man was down? General von Bernhardi's opinion of your officers of higher grade is well known."[1]

And finally, turning to English society, the indictment centres upon that movement towards Woman's Suffrage which has characterized English life during the last two years. "Does not the Suffragette, loud-voiced, coarse-minded, stealing about like a thief with a hammer up her sleeve, represent English women to the civilized world?" To this caricature they oppose the picture of the German woman, her virtues, her dignity and her simplicity. They cite the magnificent answer of the Prussian mother in the War of Liberation of 1813: "Who is the noblest woman?" "She who

---

[1] Bernhardi's opinion of our commanders is written all over his book, although he has the highest regard for the English private, for the rank and file.

has given most sons to die for the Fatherland."
Or they quote Queen Luise: "The children's
world, that is world enough for me." Yet she was
capable of appreciating Goethe. German women,
too, they assert, have gone to war; but German
women make war, not against flower-beds or golf-
links, insensate pillar-boxes or shop windows, but
like soldiers against soldiers. They quote those
tragic and pathetic incidents which occurred during
the great *Befreiungskrieg* exactly a hundred years
ago; and from that they go back four years earlier
to those incidents which marked the battlefields in
the heroic rising of the Prussian Schill in 1809,
when in more than one instance, as the helmets of
the dead were removed, a flood of golden hair
rolled down from under the helmet to the waist of
the fallen. *That*, they say, is how German women
go to war.

Now the accuracy or inaccuracy of the various
counts in this indictment is irrelevant here; what
concerns us is that, now on this point, now on that,
it is accepted by thousands of Germans at the
present day as a fair portraiture of England and
the English. All Germans do not subscribe to all
these counts, few Germans do not subscribe to
some. It is vain to call this an echo of the Boer
War; the longest echo does not last twelve years.
Besides, what is more evident to history than that
there was some deeper cause than Wilhelm II's
telegram for that extraordinary outburst of hate?

The significance of this indictment is its moral scorn. And the inference drawn from it may be stated thus: How is the persistence of a great unwarlike Power sprawling Fafnir-wise across the planet to be tolerated by a nation of warriors? Ought not the arrogated world-supremacy of such a race to be challenged? He who strikes at England does not necessarily sin against the light or commit a crime against humanity. England is failing because she ought to fail. She is already straining to the utmost. This she betrays by her pleadings with Germany to disarm. Why should not Belgium or Paraguay, for that matter, propose to Germany to limit her armaments? How did England act towards Denmark in 1801 or again in 1807? There you have the epitome of the entire history of England. But now that she feels her strength leaving her, now that her day is over, she talks to others of disarmament! It is the first time in history that such propositions have been made, and it is fitting enough that they should come from this hypocrite power. England may gradually sink from internal decay, as Venice gradually sank after 1500, dying of senility, until at a touch from Napoleon's sword she crumbled; or, if she has spirit enough, England may perish from a bayonet-thrust to the heart. But perish she must. And the judgment of the great national historian of Germany is quoted—Heinrich von Treitschke, a man whose position is almost as if he were the

poet-laureate in prose of Bismarckism and of the
Hohenzollern dynasty. In Treitschke's phrase, "a
thing that is wholly a sham cannot in this universe
of ours endure for ever. It may endure for a day,
but its doom is certain; there is no room for it in a
world governed by valour, by the Will to Power."
And it was of England that he spoke.

V

THE prophecy of Niebuhr eighty years ago, the
fall of Britain which Stein in his dying years
augured, is thus for these critics nearer fulfilment.
The mode of the fulfilment is uncertain.

The question of questions to young Germans,
eager with historical analogies, exuberant with
life, is: Who is to be the inheritor of this moribund, or quasi-moribund, empire? This Venice-
Carthage of the twentieth century—who is to
destroy her?

No one who has studied Russian political history,
Russian art and literature, the evolution of Russian
ideas, no one who has witnessed the pathetic
uncouth attempts of the Duma, can possibly see in
Russia a world-leader. That part France has
played, and cultured Germans join with Nietzsche
in their tribute to the *past* services of France to
humanity. She gave her name to the Crusaders;
in the sixteenth century she brought Italy to
Europe; in the eighteenth she was a legislator in

thought. Napoleon in 1809 attempted to wrench a planet from the hideous tentacles of this octopus, this British dominion strangling a world. Napoleon failed to achieve this deliverance of the planet from what Heine called the dullest, most insufferable, commonplace and *bourgeois* of all empires. Shall Germany succeed in that task of world-liberation?

To the students of Sybel, who, awed and solemn, saw in 1870 the manifest finger of God; to the students of Giesebrecht, who saw in Germany the nation of nations, God's chosen for the accomplishment of His inscrutable will, the answer is obvious; and when from the writings of Giesebrecht they turn to Treitschke, and from Treitschke to Droysen and Häusser, the old crude idea of a day of reckoning with England acquires a new significance. Germany is watching and waiting. Year by year silently she prepares. She recalls the alternate elations and trembling counsels in Rome before the march of Alaric in the fifth century; and with warrior-laughter she measures the certainty of her triumph by the convulsive panic-attacks of her ignoble foe! After all, on this earth the one thing that is insufferable, whether in politics or in religion, whether in private or in national affairs, is that a sham should go on pretending to be a reality, that weakness should persist in grimacing as power, falsehood as truth, injustice as justice. That is the hypocrisy of the soul. Hateful to God and to the enemies of God is such continuance—"A Dio spiacenti ed a' nemici sui!"

And when from the present and the nearer past Germans turn to the remoter past and to the distant periods of their history and inquire: "What are *our* title-deeds to world-empire?" a series of heroic and tragic forms meets their wondering eyes. For Englishmen, indifferent to or careless of their own history and blankly ignorant of Germany's, it is difficult to realize the effect upon the German mind of the discovery of the imperial eras of her history—the recovery of Charlemagne as a German hero, the exhumation from chronicle and annals of the forms of the Ottonides, and, above all, of the Hohenstaufen in the coloured and entrancing pages of Giesebrecht. There is no resisting the impressive grandeur of these figures, and the young German does not exist who can look back on that history without emotion and swelling pride.[1]

The Prussian School of historians has written the history of Germany as the exposition of a single divine idea—the movement towards unity under Prussia, and the creation, not of a new empire, but

[1] No one has felt more intimately than Wilhelm II. the glamour of those eras. Personally, and in his own temper, he has responded to its literary expression—the heroic *élan* of Wolfram, the naïve charm of Walther, Gottfried's wayward imaginings, the forest-romance of *Iwein*. Yet he is no mere "Cultur-König," no Ludwig of Bavaria.

of a new phase of empire. To them avatar succeeds avatar. The Karlings represent the triumph over Rome. Charlemagne ends the work begun on the obscure and bloody fields of Campi Raudii and guided to a more glorious issue by Alaric and Ataulf, by Genseric and Theodoric. The Saxons submit to the Rome-idea, to Galilee; but with the Hohenstaufen German genius in religion, in politics, in law, in poetry, asserts itself. An immense pause follows, ending in the obscurantist Habsburgs; but through all the nation's life advances.

And now, under the Hohenzollern, what is the future? Bernhardi, at least, is explicit: "For us there are two alternatives and no third—world-dominion or ruin, *Weltmacht oder Niedergang*." It is the interpretation of Treitschke's maxim, "Selbst ist der Mann."

VI

WHEN, turning to England, I consider the apathy or the stolid indifference of the nation—when, for instance, I consider the deliberate and hostile silence or loud calumnies which, for the past seven years, have accompanied Lord Roberts's crusade; and when, over against this apathy, I survey in this month of February, 1913, the energy, the single, devoted purposefulness throbbing everywhere throughout Germany, her forward-ranging effort, her inner life, her army, her fleet, I seem to hear again the thunder of the footsteps of a great host. . . . It is the war-bands of Alaric!

And pondering the future, seeking in the past, where alone it can be found, some taper-light to illumine the future, there rises before me one of the most solemn moments that I have ever personally experienced in English history. It was in 1900, in the early stages of the Boer War. But a few weeks ago, and the Scythian's taunt to the Roman Cæsar seemed borne to us down the centuries, "I marvel that you still speak of empire, you who can no longer make war upon a village!" Now the crisis was over.

On that afternoon we had before us in the Albert Hall a great statesman, the late Marquis of Salisbury. What had been in *his* mind during the fateful weeks? And as he rose and the immense hush swept over the audience it was difficult not to recall Milton's verses, born perhaps of his own recollection of some chance visit to the House when Strafford rose or Pym, or from later memories of Cromwell himself:

". . . . with grave
Aspect he rose, and in his rising seem'd
A pillar of state; deep on his front engraven
Deliberation sat and publick care;
And princely counsel in his face yet shone
Majestick, though in ruin; sage he stood

With Atlantean shoulders fit to bear
The weight of mightiest monarchies; his look
Drew audience and attention still as night
Or summer's noontide air, while thus he spake."

In Lord Salisbury, at once in his personality and
in his genius, I saw then, as I see now, the greatest
statesman in English history since the eighteenth
century, the last great Englishman of the line of
Strafford, Somers, Bolingbroke, Carteret, Chat-
ham and Canning. Certainly in no politician in
English history have we the proofs of a profounder
insight. In this very matter of Germany, for
instance, he foresaw, point by point, her development; and at the beginning of his career, in one
brilliant article after another in our quarterlies,
Lord Salisbury, then Lord Robert Cecil, marked
out the exact lines which that development of
Germany took—from the Kiel Canal right on to
those batteries and "Dreadnoughts" concentrated
there in the North Sea, which are already, whether
we regard them as such or not, the first conflict
between England and Germany.[1]

And in delivering one of the last and, I think, one
of the greatest of his speeches, Lord Salisbury must

[1] And in that conflict England has suffered her first defeat, her
first moral defeat. She has had to withdraw her fleet from the
Mediterranean. That sea was once ours—an English lake. It is
no longer ours. Our power is concentrated, watching our dearest
friends, those Germans who have no intention whatever of coming
near England!

have felt the futility of his insight. He might, if Greek tragedy had been as familiar to him as the laws of metals, have cited the verses of Teiresias:

Φεῦ Φεῦ, Φρονεῖν ὡς δεινὸν ἔνθα μὴ τέλη
λύη Φρονοῦντι.[1]

The thought must have been in his mind. Yet he was to the last a fighter, an Englishman who never doubted his country's ultimate victory, temperate, a master of the under-statement, a man whom, upon the whole, it is a greater achievement for a nation to have produced than to have produced a Bismarck.[2]

And the words which Lord Salisbury spoke that day? If ever a great warning was given to a people it was contained in those words, in his reference to dying empires and dying nations, to the passing of kingdoms, the vicissitudes of States and

[1] "Alas, how dreadful to have wisdom where it profits not the wise!"

[2] I do not find less vividness, more wordiness in his speeches than in those of Bismarck. Eulogizers of an academic bias, indeed, assert that Bismarck's speeches will endure whilst Germany endures. He has enriched, they say, the German language with innumerable phrases; but when challenged they are slow to produce those phrases. They begin and nearly always end with "blood and iron." I make no such claims for Lord Salisbury. He was not an artist, nor was Bismarck; but he was superior to the latter as a thinker. Had he been a German he would not have incurred the just and savage contempt which Otto Weininger and Nietzsche have poured on Bismarck.

the mutation in things; and, above all, in his appeal
to Englishmen to arm and prepare themselves for
war, for a war which might be on them at any hour,
and a war for their very existence as a nation and
as a race. And he quoted with deep meaning and
deep purpose—for as an orator Lord Salisbury
seldom strayed into the past of history without
meaning to the utmost every word he said—he
quoted the downfall of Carthage. [1]

As I walked from the meeting, the twilight falling across the Park, the words of another orator
came back to me—the exhortation addressed by
Demosthenes to Athens, words which, spoken in
Athens' darkest hour, bear a strange resemblance to
those spoken by Lord Salisbury in this, the last of
his great speeches. "Yet, O Athenians," said the
Greek, "yet is there time! And there is one
manner in which you can recover your greatness,
or, dying, fall worthy of your past at Marathon
and Salamis. Yet, O Athenians, you have it in
your power; and the manner of it is this. Cease to

[1] Underlying the discussions in this country as to Germany's
motives for war with England there is often the assumption that
it is not England that Germany desires, but England's colonies.
Yet has England the power to surrender the colonies?   Or if she
surrendered them, Canada or New Zealand, for instance, would
they yield at England's bidding?   And in attempting to enter
into possession of Canada, Germany would at once find herself at
war with the United States. But it is *not* our colonies that Germany desires. It is a great central European State, with these
islands as its conquered provinces—that is the true meaning of
Lord Salisbury's last solemn warnings from the fate of Carthage.

hire your armies. Go yourselves, every man of you, and stand in the ranks; and either a victory beyond all victories in its glory awaits you, or, falling, you shall fall greatly and worthy of your past!"

The rôles of Demosthenes in Athens and of Cato or Tacitus in Rome are significant. These men are phenomena in an onward-rushing stream. But Athens listened to Demosthenes as she might have listened to the protagonist in one of the tragedies. Yet this was her own tragedy. Would England be wiser than Athens?

Twelve years have passed. The voice which that afternoon thrilled an immense audience is still. Edward VII has succeeded, and, after a brief dominion, has followed the Empress-Queen to the vaults at Windsor. It was 1900; it is 1913; and to the words of the last great Englishman in politics there have been added the message and solemn warning of perhaps the greatest living leader of men in the field of battle, the man who more than any other merits the name "the Sidney of these later times"—Lord Roberts. How much more insistent at this hour, how much more imperious, challenging to every Englishman who cares for more than the day's transient interests, have become the words of the Greek orator, which find this strange echo, after more than two thousand years, in the summons of these great Englishmen: "Rouse yourselves from your lethargy! Cease to

hire your soldiers! Arm and stand in the ranks
yourselves—as Englishmen should! And thus,
dying you shall die greatly, or, victorious, yours
shall be such a victory as nothing in England's
past can exceed or rival."

LECTURE II

PEACE AND WAR

I

THE theme of our last lecture was the confrontation of two great nations, each endowed from the past with the memories of ancient valour, of heroism in art and poetry as in war and politics; each, again, possessing that attribute which I can only describe as innate capacity or genius for empire. Yet the one has been for two hundred years the possessor of the richest as well as the most interesting portions of this earth, whilst the other is shut within its boundaries, the Baltic, the Danube, and the Rhine. England is a nation schooled in empire from the past, the power which once belonged to the few gradually passing more and more into the ranks of the English race itself, so that you have for the first time in history at once a nation and a democracy that is imperial.[1]

[1] This is the unique character of Britain as an empire. Athens was an example of this, but Athens was a civic empire, not a national empire in the sense in which England is a nation. Moreover, whilst it was in form a republic and democratic, it was in its essence aristocratic and oligarchic, the large majority of the population having no share, direct or indirect, in government.

46

In contrast to this, Germany is a nation which is undisciplined in empire, which has never yet known its glory. The position of Wilhelm II is that of an emperor without an empire.

And the question we had to consider, quite abstractly, was: What, according to the philosophy of history, or even according to the mere processes of common sense, is likely to result from such a confrontation? Above all, what is likely to result when the first nation, though pursuing colossal organic ideals, yet seems to have become almost weary of the glory of empire, expressing frequently the desire for arbitration, for the limitation of armaments, a "naval holiday," peace at any price;[1] when its war-spirit, its energy, its sense of

---

The nearest approach to Athens is not England, but the Venice of the middle period, the Venice of the great Serrata del Consiglio, where the whole mass of the inhabitants were excluded from political power, unless those descended from or connected with the governing authorities of the time.

[1] Within the last few days, for instance, at a mere suggestion by Admiral Tirpitz as to the diminution of the German Navy, the whole Liberal Press rushed forward like gudgeons to welcome even the shadow of a pretence of peace. Yet what really underlay this suggestion was the desire of the German government to have the more power to put forward their unprecedented demand for fifty-two millions to increase the German Army. But, indeed, to no student of German history, above all to no student of Hohenzollern history, does this give the slightest surprise. Such Machiavellism in politics has been the mark of Prussian history from the moment that Prussia appeared as a first-rate Power in Europe under the Great Elector, when it led to Prussia's first great victory at Fehrbellin. What was the policy of Frederick I

heroism are apparently diminishing, and the mere craving for life and its comforts seems to be conquering every other passion—as if to this nation the aim of all life were the avoidance of suffering— what, I say, is likely to result, if, confronting this, you have a nation high in its courage, lofty in its ambitions, containing within itself apparently inexhaustible forces, moving on its own path, which in the future may lead it to destinies to which even the imagination of a Treitschke can hardly assign a limit?

In to-day's lecture we have a somewhat different problem to face, but one that is intimately and organically connected with the subject of the last lecture. It is the problem indicated by such phrases as "universal peace," "the end of war," "all our swords turned to reaping-hooks, all our barracks turned to granaries," and the like, the problem raised by those who would wish those energies which now find their scope in battle to be diverted to ends which have as their object that great aim in life—the avoidance of suffering and

---

and of Frederick the Great himself but just this? "He is a fool," said Frederick the Great, "and that nation is a fool, who, having the power to strike his enemy unawares, does not strike and strike his deadliest." Even Frederick William III, empty and vain as he was, a man whom Napoleon derided as "a tailor amongst kings," used this same policy in 1813 against Napoleon —and the Battle of the Nations was the result. And in the nineteenth century the same policy has guided the Emperor William I and the present Kaiser.

the multiplication of comforts; in a word, the problem of Pacificism and the theories of the Pacificists and their comparative influence on England and on Germany.

The theory of Pacificism is a growing force in English thought and English literature, and is, in English politics, apparently becoming a principle of a great and historical party—one of its ideals, at least. We have in practical politics witnessed its operation during the last decade in the noisy if transient enthusiasm, not necessarily insincere, with which the successive Conferences at The Hague have been garlanded; or again in the reception of President Taft's "Message"; or again in the appeals to arbitration, and the various proposals for the limitation of armaments, serious or grotesque, to which I have referred.

In this effusive sentiment for peace, these spasmodic efforts to stop what it names "the mad race for armaments," has England, this Power which possesses one-fifth of the globe and an army at least as large as that of Switzerland, forgotten its sense of humour? Do we imagine that the other Powers of the Continent see England exactly as England sees itself—England! the successful burglar who, an immense fortune amassed, has retired from business, and having broken every law, human and divine, violated every instinct of honour and fidelity on every sea and on every continent, desires now the protection of the police!

4

"If you are not a coward," says a character in one of the Sagas, "stand still whilst I send you this gift"—the hurling of a spear! Similarly Germany retorts when England, under her hypocritical or anxious dread, proposes to disarm—"You are the great robber-State; yet now in the twentieth century, as if the war for the world were over because you are glutted with booty, now it is you, you who preach to us Germans universal peace, arbitration, and the diminution of armaments! But our position is that this war is *not* over." And they exhibit England's overtures to Germany as due to subtlety or cowardice.

That is the significance of Germany's reply to the offer of the British government in 1907 to reduce her programme from three "Dreadnoughts" to two. Her answer was to increase her estimates and accelerate her programme. That is the significance of her answer in 1908, when England laid down only two "Dreadnoughts" and Germany retorted by laying down four. That, above all, is the significance of Germany's action in 1911, when, amid all the froth and loathsome sentiment and empty vapouring around President Taft's "Message"—when it seemed as if humanity, in politics, at least, had forgotten its own semblance— suddenly a man's voice, human at last, announced itself in the courage and common-sense of Beth-mann-Hollweg's utterance (March, 1911), "The vital strength of a nation is the only measure of that nation's armaments." And that, in 1913, is still the significance of Germany's answer to the egregious proposal of "a naval holiday": a war levy of £52,000,000 to be expended on fortresses, aircraft, and barracks; the peace strength of the army to be raised from six hundred thousand to between eight and nine hundred thousand men.

Germany will never sincerely cease arming. If England builds on the dream of Germany acquiescent she is destined to a bloody and terrible awakening. Bethmann-Hollweg, in 1911, but repeats the truth enunciated by Treitschke in 1890, that a nation's armed force is the expression of a nation's will to power, of a nation's will to life, and must advance with that life. We can understand the elation of Bernhardi, his pride in his country and its great past, his belief in its yet greater future as the nation of nations, dowered with the right to set itself the high task of guiding the future of humanity.

A year ago, in speaking of the French Revolution, I defined the essence of that movement as the strife from a high to an ever higher reality. Amongst the Powers and States of the Continent and of the world that seems Germany's part at the present hour.

And here let me say with regard to Germany that of all England's enemies she is by far the greatest; and by "greatness" I mean not merely magnitude, not her millions of soldiers, her millions of inhabitants, I mean grandeur of soul. She is the greatest and most heroic enemy—if she *is* our enemy—that England, in the thousand years of her history, has ever confronted. In the sixteenth century we made war upon Spain and the empire of Spain. But Germany in the twentieth century is a greater power, greater in conception, in thought, in all that makes for human dignity, than was the Spain of Charles V and Philip II. In the seventeenth century we fought against Holland; but the Germany of Bismarck and the Kaiser is greater than the Holland of De Witt. In the eighteenth century we fought against France; and again, the Germany of to-day is a higher, more august power than France under Louis XIV.

II

WHAT, then, is Pacificism? Dismissing from our minds for a moment German criticism or German interpretation of England's purposes, let us consider the ideal itself and its exponents.

The ideal in itself is so fair, this vision of a desirable life, that we are silent even before the eccentricities or fatuities of its advocates. Man, in his war against the vast sorrow of existence and necessary pain, declares: Now we shall at least cease to torture each other; man shall no longer add deliberately to the sufferings of man, more tiger than the tiger. This earth then shall afford the picture which allured the imagination of Milton and of Shelley, nation side by side with nation, race beside race, arranged in variegated communities and States—monarchies, empires, democracies, republics—sedulous in a many-coloured harmonious activity. The very memory of war and of war-heroisms—Napoleon, Cæsar, Alexander, Achilles—falls into the dim background of an ever remoter past from which humanity has liberated itself, dedicated, not to war, but to the emulous rivalries of peace, to the creation of beauty, to the perfecting of the mind, to the discovery of fresh modes of access to human nobility and to human joy—music, painting, sculpture, poetry, architecture; dedicated to the concentration in peace and leisure of man's faculties upon the extension of knowledge, the conquest of the eras of the past and of the eras of the future as it bursts through the present and its veils like the sun through fogs, the ever wider expansion of our scrutiny into the interstellar spaces, thought and imagination fusing themselves, above all, in some newer vision of the universe and of God which shall as far transcend the old philosophies and the old religions as the theories of modern astronomy transcend those of Hipparchus or Tycho Brahé.

Before such an ideal we are disposed, I say, to be tolerant even to the extravagances of Tolstoï, his appeals to the Gospels, for instance—though a dissertation upon Christ as a strategist might have been written by a mediævalist, if strategy had been an art then—and to listen without smiling when the great Spanish legist Alberdi declares that the soldier is no higher than the executioner, though one would have imagined that the difference between the hangman on the scaffold, pinioning his victim before destroying him, and the warrior on the battlefield, perilling his life, would have been apparent even to a Spanish *doctrinaire!*

It is difficult to answer the contentions of Pacificism just as it is difficult to answer all modern *isms*, because every *ism* has certain groups within it, and every group offers its own interpretation. To the group represented by Count Lyof Tolstoï, for instance, war is condemnable because it is contrary to the very spirit—as *he* understands them—of the four Gospels and of religion itself. Did not Christ come to the earth to proclaim peace? Eighteen hundred years have rolled away and there is nothing but war. To this there is the retort that, though Christ does not disdain to use a metaphor from the life of camps, yet He accompanies it by no anathema on war. And the peace which Christ came to proclaim was not the peace of the ending of battles; it was the peace within the soul, the spirit at one with itself, Islâm, in the sense that Mohammed used it, a metaphysical peace altogether apart from political peace.

Then, again, another group represents war as wholly evil because it is contrary to Law, asserting that when two nations go to war it is as if two litigants in a Court of Law were to maintain each his own cause by violence. This is the position taken up by the followers of Alberdi. Yet the litigant appeals to something higher than himself, while no free State sees anything higher than itself.

Again, there is a whole crowd, to whom I need not refer individually, of lesser names, publicists, journalists, novelists and mere cranks, to whom this phantasm appears the one thing worthy to concern men in any serious manner—all of them having the peculiar characteristic that they approach the plain man, the man in the street, with a slightly truculent air: "Now, why don't you help us to bring about this good of ours?" And there is nothing for the plain man to answer unless this: "The thing you are trying to bring about does not exist—it is simply a nothing. If, as Bismarck did at the Congress of Berlin, you attempt to bring about peace between any two individual nations, that, of course, is a matter within the scope of common sense; but this other— this 'universal peace'—what is it?" And then they can only reiterate their belief in the passing away of war, when all our swords shall be turned to reaping-hooks, our barracks into granaries, and, I suppose, all our howitzers into fire-irons!

But what can be said in answer to the pacificists' minute descriptions of the horrors of war? To

throw wide the field-hospitals and exhibit doctors
and dressers at work on the wounded; to point to
the dead and dying hurried into the trenches; to
assert, "This is war; this is reality," is as convinc-
ing and as reasonable as to point to a regiment on
parade with band playing and colours flying and to
say: "*This* is the reality." War will never be
abolished by such denunciation of isolated features. For in war there is always a series of intricate and complex phenomena, extending from
the period of apparent peace to the inception of
the idea of conflict, on through the corresponding
changes in the mind and purposes of the government and nation to the conflict itself, the battle-
field, the sequel, the terms.

There in its specious and glittering beauty the
ideal of Pacificism remains; yet in the long march
of humanity across thousands of years or thousands of centuries it remains still an ideal, lost in
inaccessible distances, as when first it gleamed
across the imagination. It has always been there.
We find its traces in the Iliad and in the Sagas,
in the verse of Pindar and in the profound and
reflective prose of Thucydides. Livy's imagination responded to it, even when with the brush of
a Veronese or of a Titian he painted the wars of
Rome. It informs some of the noblest passages
of the Annals of Tacitus. It appears as the
"Truce of God" in the Middle Age, and in the
orators of the Reformation pronounces a maledic-

tion upon him who wages war unjustly. In the seventeenth century it is proclaimed as an ideal in the name of Religion, in the eighteenth in the name of Humanity, and in the nineteenth in the name of commerce, industrialism and the progress of the working classes.

It is not, perhaps, until the eighteenth century that this idea of universal peace displays its present characteristics. At the period of the Marlborough wars there appears in France a portentous folio volume by the Abbé de St. Pierre, having for its central thesis the evils of war in the abstract. The position there taken up is not very different from the position taken up by Tolstoï. War is stigmatized as being in itself hostile to religion, and is denounced as being contrary to the commands of Christ. This book produced a great many works of a similar kind, and many refutations.

In the course of the nineteenth century you find this idea appearing here in England in a new phase, above all in the "Manchester School." War is now regarded and described not so much as hostile to religion, not so much as hostile to the commands of Christ, but as inimical to the interests of industry. The peace of the world must be secured, indeed; but it is to be secured not by religion but by a great conspiracy—or co-operation, if you like —of all the forces of industry throughout Europe. That is the Manchester doctrine of universal peace—highly characteristic, one would say, of the

nineteenth century! Yet it had a distinct power
at once in France and in Germany.

The final form that this strange theory has
assumed is that which it now affects to wear in
the twentieth century, a form equally interesting.
Now war is declaimed against and universal peace
with all its beauties is proclaimed, not because war
is contrary to the laws of God, to the laws of
religion, but—because it is opposed to social well-
being, and, economically, is profitless alike to victor and to vanquished. It has ceased to pay,
and it has ceased, therefore, to add to the comfort
of nations!

Yet despite this hubbub of talk down all the
centuries war has continued—absolutely as if not a
word had been said either on one side or the other.
Man's dreadful toll in blood has not yet all been
paid. The human race bears still this burden.
Declaimed against in the name of religion, in the
name of humanity, in the name of profit-and-loss,
war still goes on, and to this day it is there—there
in the Balkans, raging at this hour!

III

WHY, then, is universal peace still an ideal? Why
is it less like some hope of the future, gilding the
eastern horizon, than like some memory of a
Saturnian age sunk far below the darkened hori-
zons of the past?

An enumeration of the evils that attend man's life in time of peace is obviously no answer. It is equally no answer to celebrate the opportunities to good-fellowship and self-sacrifice which the battle-field affords, and sometimes witnesses. Towards other ideals man has progressed—in his war against disease, for instance, and in his war against nature, the forest, the sea, the vicissitudes of season and of climate; towards this ideal alone he has made no progress. And yet it is an ideal which, unlike perennial youth or immunity from pain and disease, appears to be within his power.

War has changed its forms. Tribal forays have ceased, and the internecine hatred of clans; but the tribes and clans have themselves been merged in the higher unity of the nation or the race, and the warfares of the clan and the tribe have seemed to add all their complexity and ferocity to the wars of nations. That peculiar form of heroic warfare of the Sagas has disappeared; but the conditions of life which made it possible or necessary no longer exist. Wars between city and city, as those between Genoa and Pisa, Athens and Sparta, have also ceased; but civic States have vanished. Again, the wars of religion have ceased; but religion is no longer the dominant force in man's life. War remains as the supreme act of the State, unchanged in essence, though varying in mode. In Europe, which really governs the planet, every advance in politics or religion has been attended by war.

Now if one turns for a moment from the ideal of universal peace—whether one regards it as a mere chimera or as coming within the sphere of practical politics—to the ideal of war, its history is certainly illuminating.

To the great historians of Greece, to Thucydides, for instance, the stern disciplinarian of humanity, βίαιος διδάσκαλος, the most grave, the most tragic and the most philosophic of all historians, war represents a permanent factor in human life, and not only a permanent factor, but a noble factor. It is the school of heroism, the exercise-ground of nations, disciplining them in the highest manhood —in valour. And this attitude of the Greek historian governs equally the later Greek writers, such as Polybius, who come within the dominion of Rome. For war is at the root of Roman history. The Romans are the great inventors in the art of war; they are the first scientists in war; and to the Romans it was not a mortal man but a god that invented the formation of the Roman legion.

This attitude of Rome persists down to the Middle Age—though then, in the Middle Age, war receives the added glamour of religion. To Mohammed and to his Arabs in the East war is not only in itself a heroism, it is the divine act. And in the West, similarly, in the same period, you find the Roman Papacy adopting as the very central thought of its foreign policy a great religious war— the war of the Crusades. And if at that time you do find arising in Europe the notion of the "Truce of God," this Truce of God becomes simply the institution of a temporary peace between the feudal chiefs and barons; it is no repudiation of war in itself.

The same point of view is maintained right on to the Renaissance and Reformation period. To such a thinker and writer as Machiavelli, perhaps the most profound mind that Italy ever produced, far wider in its range of knowledge and speculation than Dante's, war is the school of *virtù*, of valour, heroism, excellence of any kind. With the Reformation, on the other hand, a more psychological investigation of war sets in. By the very spirit of the Reformation the Divine was declared to be here upon the earth, within man's reach and life, and in all human actions—man's life on earth being now not simply regarded as evil. War therefore had to receive a closer examination and an attempt had to be made to harmonize it with what seemed to be the Divine. It is then that the distinction arises between just and unjust wars. A great cause, a good cause, it was said, justifies war in the abstract; but he who wages "an unjust war," in the phrase of Grotius, endures all the responsibility for all the vile actions, all the suffering, appertaining to that war.

Frederick the Great, he who above all men exemplified heroism in war in the creation of that War-State of Prussia which has gradually grown into the German Empire of the present hour, writes in extreme age to Voltaire a letter which may be taken as the summing-up of this tedious debate: "I am old, cheerful, gouty, good-humoured. Now that Poland has been settled by a little ink and a pen, the 'Encyclopédie' cannot declaim against mercenary brigands. For the future I cannot vouch. Running over the pages of history, I see that ten years never pass without a war. This intermittent fever may have moments of respite, but cease, never!" This is the last word of the eighteenth century upon the dream of universal peace, a word spoken by one of the greatest kings of any age.

Here, then, we are brought up sharply against the question: "Is man's failure to realize the ideal of universal peace an arraignment of his capacity or his sincerity? Has he the power to realize it or is it the will that is lacking?" Without attempting further analysis and discussion, I am obliged to answer that a survey of world-history—India, Babylon, Persia, China, Hellas, Rome, the Middle Age and Modern Europe—enforces the conclusion that hitherto man has lacked not only the power but the will to end war and to establish peace throughout the continents of the habitable globe.

IV

Now it is a question surely worth considering: Why is it and for what reward that man still

clings to war? Is there anything in war that is
not wholly evil? Or must we be accused of per-
petual self-contradiction and blindness to our own
interests, all down the long six thousand years of
history? Or, on the other hand, is there in war
something which has escaped the examination of
Pacificism, and on what ground can one maintain
that this is so?

First of all, let me remind you that in human
life as a whole there are always elements and
forces, there are always motives and ideals, which
defy the analysis of reason—mysterious and dark
forces. Man shall not live by bread alone! And
in war this element constantly tends to assert
itself. It assumes forms that sometimes are
dazzling in their beauty; sometimes are wrapt in
a kind of transcendental wonder; sometimes, in
appearance at least, are simply utilitarian, or
chimerical, or fantastic. But all alike have this
quality of defying reason, of eluding the grasp
of the mind when exercised in formal judgment
merely. It is easy, for example, to demonstrate
that the glory of battle is an illusion; but by the
same argument you can demonstrate that *all*
glory and life itself is an illusion and a mockery.
Nevertheless men still live and go on pursuing that
illusion and that mockery.

As an illustration of what I mean by that which
stands above reason, let me speak to you for a
moment of that incident in the Antarctic zone

which but a few weeks ago was absorbing the
imagination of every man and woman in these
islands. Let me speak to you of Captain Scott
and his heroic band, and let us consider how far
this element that transcends reason entered into
that particular heroism.

Image to yourselves that vast, that shapeless
desolation that reigns there for ever around the
austral pole, league on frost-bound league, Death's
appanage, untainted by any life eternally, not a
motion except the wild rage of the tempest or the
silent fall of ice-flakes through the windless air—a
desolation peopled by such phantoms as daunted
even the imagination of Camoens, the poet of
Vasco da Gama, the first great adventurer into
those silent seas. There, during the past year,
month by month the Polar sun forlorn has gleamed
through the mists, month by month through the
long night the Southern Cross has hung her
glittering fires on the steep blackness of the Antarctic sky, looking down upon some little heaps of
English dust. · Why have they come hither—these
Englishmen? What is the madness that has
drawn them from their secure homes in Devon-
shire or Suffolk, Ireland or the Welsh border, to
die thus agonizing here? *That* is the question
which, by not too daring a metaphor, the Southern
Cross might ask as through that long night she
looks down upon the English dead extended there
in frozen rigidity unmoving. To what possible

end have they come there?   Assuredly for no mere
utilitarian end.   The lure that has led them to
their glory and their rest is Reason indeed, the
increase of Knowledge, but something higher also.
Mere love of formal Knowledge—questions as to
the precise position of the South Pole, or whether
the fossils of an extinct race of animals which once
wandered there are preserved in the rocks and
stones—would never have inspired that drama.

For put before yourselves, incident by incident,
the later stages of that heroism—first the careful
survey on the Pole itself, hour by priceless hour
a hostage to death, then the terrible return with
the sick comrade, his death, and then that strange
heroism on the part of Captain Oates.   As a historian or at least a student of history, let me dwell
for a moment on the distinction of this valour.   In
the Icelandic Sagas of the Middle Age, which re-
flect in a very remarkable manner the English character of that time although they were not written
by Englishmen, you find a certain kind of courage
frequently delineated—the courage shown, say,
in the great fight to avenge the death of Kjartan,
where one man after another, when they have
surrounded the house where the enemy is en-
trenched, volunteers to be the first to attack the
house and meet death.   But in the death of
Captain Oates a valour of quite a different kind
displays itself.   In *that* courage you have something spiritual, mysterious, added to this other

courage of the Sagas—something which leads that
English gentleman to set forth solitary into the
terror-haunted darkness, seeking no visible enemy,
seeking only the universal enemy, to him a friend—
death, death; stumbling blindly, yet onwards and
still onwards into the night, into Annihilation,
fronting it. . . .

And then pass to the last stage in the drama—to
that other death. There in the tent beside his
dead the leader sits, still alive; there he sits, un-
vanquished and unappalled, his head propped
against the tent-pole to ease his fatigue in the last
slow dreadful vigil, whilst down over his magnifi-
cently English features a night deeper than the
Polar night descends. And what are the thoughts
which then flicker in front of him? We know
them; we have them written in his own hand in
that priceless record—priceless because authentic.
"The greatness of England—my nation!" It is
the greatness of England which uplifts him as
death steals over his features like a marble mask.

Here, surely, we have a kind of heroism which it
would daunt the courage of any pacificist, of any
doctrinaire, to explain by the profit and loss theory
or to analyze by the ordinary processes of reason
at all.

Now I suggest to you that one explanation of
this extraordinary paradox in human history—the
persistence of war in spite of what seems its un-
reason—is that there is something in war, after

all, that is analogous to this heroism there in the Antarctic zone, something that transcends reason; that in war and the right of war man has a possession which he values above religion, above industry and above social comforts; that in war man values the power which it affords to life of rising above life, the power which the spirit of man possesses to pursue the Ideal. In all life at its height, in thought, art, and action, there is a tendency to become transcendental; and if we examine the wars of England or of Germany in the past we find governing these wars throughout this higher power of heroism, or of something, at least, which transcends reason.

Until about five hundred years ago England can hardly be said to have fought as a nation. Her wars till then represent rather the heroism of dynasties and of individual groups of men than the heroism of the nation as such. But towards the middle of the fourteenth century there began a series of really national wars in England—the wars against France, with their great battles of Crecy and Agincourt, and the great disaster, the hour when with Talbot at Castillon an empire sank. Then there is the war against Spain in the sixteenth century, and in the seventeenth the wars against Holland and the France of Louis XIV, which continue into the eighteenth century and find their natural termination only in the wars against Napoleon. In the nineteenth century

there is a long series of wars in all parts of the world
—in the Crimea, in India and Afghanistan, in
China, in New Zealand, in Egypt, in Western and in
Southern Africa; so that it might be said without
exaggeration that through all these years scarcely
a sun set which did not look upon some Englishman's face dead in battle—dead for England!

Now for what have these wars been fought?
Can one detect underneath them any governing
idea, controlling them from first to last? I answer
at once: There is such an idea, and that idea is
the idea of Empire. All England's wars for the
past five hundred years have been fought for
empire. There is first of all a war for an empire in
France—a wholly unrealizable idea, a war bound
to end in failure in the very nature of things, and
yet a war to which the English nation gave itself
with a splendour of courage, a lavishness at once
of blood and treasure, that still fills the mind with
admiration and lifts it beyond those utilitarian
speculations to which I have referred.

That war ends in disaster; and just at the
moment when that disaster is most complete,
when it seems as if England were doomed to fall
to a secondary or even a tertiary place in world-
history, suddenly there occurs that event which
it is hard not to ascribe to some deeper cause than
chance, to some profounder purpose than the
hazard in things. It is the discovery of the means
to a greater empire than the empire in France, to

an empire at once in the sunrise and in the sunset. It is America: it is India. The effect of this discovery is like the awakening of a sleeper. A new hope for Englishmen arises, and now the English imagination is fired and filled with this idea, so that throughout the whole of English life, in every phase and grade of it, there is that exaltation, that spiritual exultancy which finds its supreme expression in the Elizabethan drama, in the great dramatists of that time, in Marlowe and Shakespeare and Ford, in Webster, in Beaumont and Fletcher, in that outburst of thought and of art which has no parallel in world-history—not in Greece itself, unless possibly for a moment in the age of Pericles.[1]

This war for empire again finds expression in the conflict with Spain, in the wars against Holland and France in the seventeenth and eighteenth centuries. And what was the stake for which England fought in all her battles against Bonaparte? The stake was world-empire; and Napoleon knew it well. France's opportunity was now, or her world-empire was lost for ever. Bonaparte fought for that, and fought for it titanically and superbly; and dying there in Sainte-Hélène there died with him a world-hope.

---

[1] Even there it is less rich and varied in poetry; although, on the other hand, the glory of the Parthenon, of sculpture, belongs to Greece alone. That is the inalienable and for ever precious gift of Hellas.

Here then we have this transcendental force governing the wars of England. And if we turn from England to Germany we find the same element which transcends reason governing the wars of Germany. One emperor after another is led south across the Alps in the attempt to make Italy a part of Germany; to govern Italy, and therefore the Papacy, from the Rhine; to make a reality of that which was called the "Holy Roman Empire"—an attempt doomed to disaster, just as England was doomed to disaster on the fields of France, a perfectly hopeless dream! Yet what heroism, what courage, what names! It is to those names and to that heroic past that Germans turn for inspiration as year by year this newer hope of empire arising within the German mind deepens.

This dream of empire continues in her later wars.

*　　*　　*　　*　　*　　*　　*

[NOTE.—*This section was left unfinished. A survey of the wars of Germany in the light of this idea is evidently the line on which it would have been continued, but unfortunately the lecturer left no notes which could be used to finish the section.*]

V

Now considering the wars of England and of Germany in this light, considering also the respective positions of these two nations at the present day, what is likely to be the comparative effect on England and Germany of Pacificism with its denial of the part played by danger and by suffering in all heroic life?

Upon a young and virile nation, a rising military State, daily growing in power, Pacificism can never exert much influence for evil; there is no possibility of such a nation being seriously turned from heroism. But to an old nation in which certain forces of decay *seem*, at least, already to be manifesting themselves, might not such a theory, if too ardently adopted, be fraught with very terrible danger, with very real and disastrous consequences?

In regard to Germany we are confronted by certain circumstances that indisputably merit our consideration here in England. There is, for instance, the annual appearance in Germany of very nearly seven hundred books dealing with war as a science. This points, at once, to an extreme preoccupation in that nation with the idea of war. I doubt whether twenty books a year on the art of war appear in this country, and whether their circulation, when they do appear, is much more than twenty!

There is, again, the German way of regarding war. What is the attitude of mind towards war of Treitschke, for example, a man whose spirit still controls German youth, German patriotism, a man who has a power in Germany, as a thinker and as a writer, that you might compare to the power exercised by Carlyle and by Macaulay put together in this country? To him the army is simply the natural expression of the vital forces of the nation; and just as those vital forces of the nation increase so shall the German army and the German navy increase. A nation's military efficiency is the exact coefficient of a nation's idealism. That is Treitschke's solution of the matter. His answer to all our talk about the limitation of armaments is: Germany shall increase to the utmost of her power, irrespective of any proposals made to her by England or by Russia, or by any other State upon this earth. And I confess it is a magnificent and a manly answer, an answer worthy of a man whose spirit of sincerity, of regard for the reality of things, is as great as Carlyle's.

The teaching of Treitschke's disciple, General von Bernhardi, is the same. War to him is a duty. Nothing is more terrible than the government of the strong by the weak, and war is the power by which the strong assert their dominion over the weak. War sets the balance right. And the younger poets of Germany breathe the same spirit—Liliencron, for instance, who represents most fitly that aspect of modern German literature. I have not time at this late hour to speak of him so fully as I had hoped; but that spirit of war and glory which informs his battle-sketches of the war of 1870—I can sum it up for you. It is in the verses of Goethe's Euphorion:

> "Träumt ihr den Friedenstag?
> Träume, wer träumen mag!
> Krieg ist das Losungswort!
> Sieg! und so klingt es fort."[1]

That is the spirit in which war is regarded in contemporary Germany. And I am not the least astonished that when we send over from England an itinerant preacher of universal peace to explain to Germany, "For the love of God, don't make war upon England; for it won't pay you"—I am not the least astonished that in a mass meeting of two thousand students at the university of Göttingen this itinerant preacher and all his works were set aside. How can we wonder at it?

England and Germany—on which is Pacificism likelier to exercise a deleterious and a dangerous effect? From to-day's survey of eternal abstract principles, as from last week's survey of ephemeral yet not insignificant criticism of England and her empire, it becomes apparent that Germany is not England's only enemy, perhaps not even her chief.

And yet, and yet—from those frozen regions of the South there seems to come, like a trumpet-call,

---

[1] "Dream ye of peaceful sway?
Dream on, who dream it may.
War still is empire's word!
Peace? By the victor's sword!"

the message: The greatness of England still, the greatness of England still!—England, for which men can die as these men died, with a valour that is higher than the valour of the past—a message reinforcing again those words of the Athenian which at this crisis of our fate I would to God rang in every Englishman's ears and were graven on every Englishman's heart: "Yet is there time, O Athenians, yet is there time! Cease to hire your armies; cease to fill your ranks with the off-scourings of a planet. Go yourselves and stand in the ranks; and then, dying, you shall die greatly and with a glory that shall surpass the glories of the past, or, victorious, you shall gain a victory that shall exceed all your victories in the past!"

LECTURE III

I

TOWARDS the end of last September I was staying in an hotel at a watering-place in the Midlands when, on a Tuesday evening, there came the news of the death of the German ambassador, Count Bieberstein, here in London. The incident made on me an unsual impression, for it seemed but yesterday that he had arrived amongst us, overflowing with energy, animated, versatile, a mind full of the future. His coming had instantly greatened all our political life; for, in the defect of even second-rate statesmen amongst ourselves, the presence of a man who, if he did not actually attain the first rank, certainly suggested the first rank, had given a kind of dignity and meaning to political life such as it had hardly known since the death of Lord Salisbury. Now, as by a stroke from the gods, that influence was withdrawn. The sense of magnitude was gone, and the busy mediocrity, the hustler, and the charlatan, corrupting and corrupt, again moved about in unrelieved oppressiveness. Those grave features with their Puritan severity of line we should see no more; his plans, his designs, were left an enigma. He had died before the great distaste and the great weariness had come upon him. To Bismarck and to Stein, as to Frederick the Great, life had long been infinitely contemptible, the purpose and the end of existence a hieroglyph written in mud. But Bieberstein had died under the everlasting illusion, believing that he was doing something, realizing some end, and that therefore some end could be realized.

And in the lounge after dinner, amid the gossip of the day, there came little splutters of intelligent or unintelligent comment on the event; and as I sat listening to these epitaphs a lady turned to me, and casting down her face and then casting up her eyes with a perfect expression of innate and indescribable hypocrisy, observed: "You do not say anything. Ah well, the news is, of course, sad, but we cannot perhaps altogether grieve that he was taken. He was dreadfully against England, was he not?" "Ah, madam," I answered, "the death of a great man is a loss to humanity, whatever be his antagonisms or his sympathies; and, after all, next to a true friend the possession of a great and magnanimous enemy is perhaps the most precious gift the gods can send us." She wrinkled her brows; for she imagined, I suppose, that by "the gods" I meant the Anglican bishops, and was perplexed.

An enemy of England? I am not certain that this is a just estimate of Count Bieberstein, but it is assuredly a fair description of the man concerning whom I have to speak to you this afternoon, Heinrich von Treitschke.

Almost the last time we see Treitschke, those noble features of his lit up, as they always were instantly lit up by any enthusiasm, whether of love or hate—almost the last time we really see him is on an evening in 1895, when, returned from a visit to England, he poured out to a company of friends all the vitriol of his scorn, antipathy and hate for England and for the English, enduring no word of comment or contradiction, until someone quoted to him Heine's malicious "Englische Fragmente," in which Heine discusses the question how it is that so ignoble a nation as England can possibly have produced a Shakespeare. And so the meeting ended in agreement and laughter. But all who listened to Treitschke that night seemed to hear in his words, as they had heard in his lectures again and again, the first dark roll that announces the coming dreadful storm, the coming war—the war that he regarded as simply inevitable —between these two empires, both the descendants of the war-god Odin, and yet, *because* of that, doomed to this great conflict.

Within six months Treitschke was dead.

II

How can one best present Treitschke to an English audience? How can one explain to an English audience something of Treitschke's position and the place he fills in German life right on from 1858 until his death, and to the present hour? The seventeen volumes of his collected writings on history, on literature and on the science of politics, his speeches on present-day questions and his political pamphlets, have not been translated and are therefore a sealed book to the majority of English readers.

Yet at once in his own personality and as a governing force in German thought, Heinrich von Treitschke ought to be deeply interesting to us; for more than any other single character in German political life he is responsible for the anti-English sentiment which blazed out during the Boer War, which still reigns in German society and in the German Press, which in the Reichstag reveals itself in the frigid or ironic applause with which any references to "our amicable relations with England" are greeted. The foundations of that sentiment, of course, lie deeper than the creative power of an individual intellect or will. They are, as we have seen, beyond the control of any passing generation, rooting themselves in the dark forces which determine the destinies of peoples and of the universe itself. But Treitschke, beyond any other German, stands forth as the interpreter of these forces. His interpretations have sunk deep into the German mind; his fiery challenges and impassioned rhetoric have coloured German thought. Though his greatest book deals only with the record of thirty-two years, it is spoken of *sans phrase* as "the History of Germany,"[1] and "our great national historian" has become a familiar periphrasis in newspapers and on platforms for Treitschke's name. The real and abstract principles of German history seen and reinterpreted through Treitschke's medium—that for many men in Germany has become their faith.

These are arguments of a unique and immense influence. And what are the feelings towards England which this great historian and orator expresses? He incessantly points his nation onwards to the war with England, to the destruction of England's supremacy at sea as the means by which Germany is to burst into that path of glory and of world-dominion towards which, through all the centuries of her history, she has deliberately moved. The Ottonides in the tenth century sketched the plan; it has been reserved for the Hohenzollern in the twentieth to fill in the details.

[1] The subject of Treitschke's "Deutsche Geschichte" is the transformation of the German Confederation into the Empire; but he had only reached the year 1848 when, at the age of 62, he died. His "History" may be regarded as the analogue of Pertz's "Life of Stein."

Discussing in a former lecture the question whether the persistence of war accused humanity of self-contradiction or some secular hypocrisy, I suggested that in the laws governing States and individuals the highest functions transcend utility and transcend even reason itself; that in the present stage of the world's history to end war is not only beyond man's power but contrary to man's will, since in war there is some secret possession or lingering human glory to which man clings with an unchangeable persistence, some source of inspiration which he is afraid to lose, uplifting life beyond life itself, some sense of a redeeming task which, like his efforts to unriddle the universe, for ever baffled yet for ever renewed, gives a meaning to this else meaningless scheme of things.

A Greek orator has recorded an incident in the life of the Emperor Julian, when, confronting certain Teutonic tribes along the Rhine, he remonstrated with them on their restless, predatory and warlike habits, and one of their ambassadors, answering the charge, summed up his defence with the assertion: "But in war itself we see life's greatest felicity." And five centuries of almost uninterrupted war forged the unity of England. But no English historian or thinker has spoken of war quite as Treitschke has spoken of it. I do not recollect a single passage in his writings in which the conventional regrets are expressed, or where conventional phrases such as "the scourge of mankind," "the barrier to human progress," occur as descriptions of war. From an early period in his literary career, on the other hand, phrases of a quite different order abound in his writings, phrases in which war appears, if not as "the supreme felicity of mankind," at least as a great factor in the onward strife towards perfection; whilst any attempt at its abolition is characterized as unwise and immoral.

When General von Bernhardi, in a pamphlet published in February last, ("Unsere Zukunft: ein Mahnwort an das deutsche Volk"), puts before his countrymen the alternatives of world-dominion or ruin, when he speaks of war as a biological necessity and as an extension of policy, and the manliest extension, he is expressing, perhaps not in the happiest literary manner, Treitschke's ideas. The poet Liliencron, Treitschke's contemporary, has expressed them much more happily, much more fervently; and Liliencron was a poet with a sword by his side. He fought at Königgrätz in 1866, at the age of thirty-two, and at Wörth and Mars-la-Tour in 1870. And what is a governing thought of Liliencron's battle-sketches, of "Der Richtungspunct," for instance, or of "Eine Sommerschlacht," except the thought of Faust:

"O selig der, dem er im Siegesglanze
Die blut'gen Lorbeern um die Schläfe windet."[1]

[1] "O happy he for whom in victory's splendour
Death wreathes the blood-stained laurel round his brow."

6

There is no greater contrast in literature than between the emotion which pervades Tolstoï's "War and Peace," the scene, say, on the redan in the description of Borodino, and the emotion which pervades Liliencron's descriptions of Wörth and Mars-la-Tour. And, again I must remind you, Liliencron not less than Tolstoï knew what he was talking about.

III

IN his own country Treitschke is sometimes described as the Coryphæus of the Prussian School, that group of historians of whom Droysen, Häusser and Sybel, Pertz, the biographer of Stein, and Delbrück, the biographer of Gneisenau, are perhaps the best-known names in this country. The greatness of Prussia and the fate-appointed world-task or world-mission of Germany under the sacred dynasty of the Hohenzollern is the inspiration of all these men.

Treitschke's "History" is characterized by punctilious research and by reliance on original documents and original documents only. There are brilliant chapters on literature and the interconnexion of literature and history. Here he suggests Taine, his contemporary; and, had he lived another ten years, his book might have been styled "The Foundations of Contemporary Germany." English critics have sometimes compared him with

Macaulay. Treitschke himself would have resented the comparison; for he has frequently expressed his unreserved contempt for the historian of the Revolution of 1688, arraigned his accuracy, derided his estimates of men, challenged his appreciation of facts, and stigmatized his philosophy and his outlook upon human fate. He has Macaulay's hates and prejudices, his vituperative energy; he has his power of fervent admiration. Yet as a master of words, a stylist, Treitschke is much inferior to Macaulay. His portraiture is often an accumulation of minute details which have never coalesced into a living personality. A Titian portrait beside a Bronzino—that is the quality of Macaulay's style beside Treitschke's: for instance the portraits of the Whig Junto beside those of the men in whom Frederick William IV put his trust. Treitschke at one time had wished to be a poet, and he had considerable metrical skill. Yet in speaking of poetry he is rarely a poet; and a comparison of his patriotic verses with "The Lays of Ancient Rome" is a fair measure of Treitschke's inferiority to Macaulay as a writer.[1]

[1] Nietzsche as a stylist might have taught Treitschke much; but against the creator of Zarathustra Treitschke was bitterly and irreconcilably prejudiced from the very beginning of the former's career, when Treitschke wrote of him to Overbeck as "that rum fellow Nietzsche." He even quarrelled with Overbeck because of the latter's sympathy with his young colleague at Basle. His roughness to Nietzsche in 1872 is not worse than Stein's roughness to Goethe, and arose from similar causes. Treitschke divines in

On the other hand, one may more justly compare Treitschke's immense and enduring influence, not only in Prussia but throughout the German world, with the influence exercised by Carlyle upon England since 1858.[1] And Treitschke's influence has gone on steadily increasing throughout Germany until the present day. Treitschke and Carlyle resemble each other in their high seriousness, sincerity, downrightness and deep moral strength. Do not imagine, however, that there is any *further* resemblance between them. For instance, there is not in all the seventeen volumes of Treitschke any hint of that broad human laughter which you find in very nearly every page of the thirty volumes of Carlyle. In all Treitschke I doubt whether there is a single laugh. You may say, if you like, that this is because Germany has obtained free political institutions so recently and therefore has not yet acquired the power to take them humorously!

Treitschke, observe, is nothing if not a politician.

---

the author of "Unzeitgemässe Betrachtungen" "the good European" of later works; and therefore the bad Prussian, the bad German.

[1] Carlyle was born forty years before Treitschke, but Carlyle's influence was slower in making itself felt; he was very late in coming to his own in English life, very late in acquiring his reputation. The first thing that gave Carlyle a grip upon English people was not "The French Revolution," published by him at two-and-forty, but his "Cromwell," published at fifty. Treitschke's influence at the universities dates from fifteen years after that.

Carlyle, in a sense, has no politics. Certainly England never took Carlyle's politics seriously. England listened wondering, sometimes amazed, but always reverent, to his moral teaching. Every book he wrote seemed to prove the truth of Goethe's diagnosis of his character—"a new moral force, the extent and effects of which it is impossible to predict." But England has ignored absolutely Carlyle's politics, whether in his attitude towards the American War, or again in "Shooting Niagara," or in "Latter Day Pamphlets," or in his view of the careers of Cromwell or Frederick— that exaltation of beneficent despotism. Treitschke's political principles, on the other hand— the doing of great things greatly, heroic action, the glory of war, and the day of reckoning with England—are the very essence of his power over Germany. These principles underlie some of the soundest German, and, above all, Prussian thought at the present hour, as they have for the last thirty years.

A further contrast between these two men is this. Treitschke is ethical rather than metaphysical. He has none of those dazzling gleams of profound metaphysical thought which constantly uplift Carlyle. Nor do you find in him the poetry of Nature which you find in Carlyle—that feeling which gives Carlyle the power to turn from the massacres there in the streets of Paris to the fall of the autumn evening over French meadows.

You do find, however, something of Carlyle's vivid insight into character, especially when Treitschke has the power of loving his characters (and unless a man loves his characters he should not write about them). This is noticeable in his incursions into English history, and even more in his studies of English literature. His sketch of Milton is still one of the very finest of that great man; and his sketch of Byron might quite easily be placed with that of the Spanish writer, Nuñez de Arce. But, again, that which appeals to Treitschke in Milton is the great political rebel. It is not the writer of the fourth book of "Paradise Lost," or of the first, or of the ninth, or of the eleventh; it is the author of that noble pamphlet, "The Tenure of Kings and Magistrates," which Milton sat writing in the very week when Charles I was being tried and doomed to death, Milton feeling it incumbent upon himself as an Englishman, though he is not a member of that high court of justice, to sit there day by day and night by night *trying* Charles I, as he maintained that every Englishman should try the king. So again, to Treitschke, with his deep Teutonic moral nature, it certainly is not the Byron of what, from a literary standpoint, is Byron's masterpiece, "Don Juan," nor is it the poet of "Childe Harold" that fascinates him. It is Byron's admiration and enthusiasm for liberty; and to Treitschke Byron's greatest verses are these:

"Yet, Freedom! yet, thy banner torn but flying,
Streams, like the thunderstorm, *against* the wind;
Thy trumpet voice, tho' broken now and dying,
The loudest still the tempest leaves behind."

IV

LET me now sketch rapidly the life and career of
this astonishing man.

Like many notable Germans of the nineteenth
century, above all that German who is now beginning to arrest the attention even of Englishmen—
for as a rule it takes at least half a century for any
true German thought to cross the North Sea!—
like Friedrich Nietzsche, and perhaps like Ranke
himself, Heinrich von Treitschke was Slavonic
in origin. His ancestors were Czechs who mi-
grated from Bohemia during the turmoils of the
Thirty Years' War and, seeking refuge from the
Jesuit plague, found security under the Protestant
Electors of Saxony. During the eighteenth century they gradually rose in the favour of the ruling
House. Under the last Elector of Saxony a
Treitschke became a Privy Councillor. He sent
his sons into the army, secured for them in 1821
the syllable *von*, and before his death had the
pride or the vanity of seeing one of them command-
ant of the fortress of Königstein, which still rises
in grey and impressive solitude on its tall rock
above the Elbe. This was Eduard von Treitschke,
the historian's father.

Treitschke was born at Dresden in September, 1834, one of the darkest and most disconsolate periods in modern German history. The old ideals were sinking; the new had not yet arisen. The despotism of Metternich lay like a dead hand upon Austria and the South; the princes clung to their privileges; Frederick William III still reigned in Prussia. Schelling died that year, sunk in obscurantism; Arndt was a professor at Bonn; Tieck had ceased to write; Wilhelm von Humboldt still lived in honourable retirement at Schloss Tegel; but Goethe had died two years before, and, a year earlier than Goethe, Hegel and Niebuhr had both passed away; Stein had died some months after Niebuhr in solitude and estrangement from his times, seeing not only Germany but Europe itself rushing upon the abyss. Schleiermacher preached for the last time in 1834. The heroes of the War of Liberation were long dead, or lived, an embarrassment and a reproach, amid a generation which, apathetic and indifferent, half wished to forget their heroism. Scharnhorst had died of his wounds at Prague (1813), in the very hour of Germany's glory; Blücher, in 1819; Yorck in 1830; and Gneisenau (just when entering upon the Polish campaign), a Field-Marshal at last, had died in 1831, like Hegel, of cholera, then raging throughout Europe. Who was there left to represent the past splendours? And in the deep night there was not a star to hint the coming dawn.

Such was the world into which Treitschke was born.[1]

In his childhood everything seemed to mark him out as a Saxon, as destined, that is to say, to follow a career in that country. Treitschke, however, early discovered something that alienated him from the career contemplated for him by his father. His mother, who was of pure German origin, was a reader of Willibald Alexis, above all of those tales the scenes of which were placed in the heroic times of Frederick the Great; and when Treitschke's own tastes began to form they led him as instinctively to the Wars of Liberation as Rousseau's tastes had led him to Plutarch, or Mirabeau's to Livy or the Rome of the Gracchi and of Sulla. He took to the study of history; and he discovered in that study the conduct of Saxony in the past, the conduct of the Saxon dynasty—perhaps the stupidest royal House in Europe. He discovered the part played by Saxony at Leipzig, and the yet more despicable part played at Waterloo; and all that was German as distinct from all that was particularist in that history took possession of his imagination.

While he was still a boy his great heroes were not the heroes of Saxony; they were all Prussians. Just as in the eighteenth century the men of the French Revolution found their inspiration in the

[1] Treitschke himself has described this period in the third volume of his "Deutsche Geschichte."

heroes of Plutarch, Caius Marius and Sulla and
Brutus, so Treitschke found his inspiration in the
Prussian heroes *à la* Plutarch, in those magnificent
figures which fill and adorn the pages of Prussian
history between 1809 and 1813. His heroes are
Gneisenau, Blücher's aide-de-camp, he who really
controlled Blücher's actions in all matters of
diplomacy; and Scharnhorst, of whom he has left
one of the most powerful sketches that German
literature possesses. Again, his hero is Stein, or
the philosopher Fichte, or Moritz Arndt the poet,
the son of a serf, author of the famous song,
"Was ist des Deutschen Vaterland?" And there is
significance as well as authenticity in the anecdote
which depicts him as a boy of fifteen reading aloud
in the presence of Beust, one of Metternich's most
repulsive satellites, an essay in the dithyrambic
manner rejoicing in the downfall of the princes
and exalting German unity, a unity which is to be
accomplished "by a race into whose blood has
passed in their youth the free and bracing winds of
the Baltic strand."

It is while he is a boy also that there overtakes
him a disaster which tries the steel and stoicism
in him. He has described it for us in a volume of
verses published in 1856—the coming upon him of
a fever, his slow recovery, and, at last, his astonish-
ment at the persistent sorrow on his mother's face,
despite his recovery. He describes his being taken
out into the garden on an early summer's day,

lying on a bench in the sun, seeing the bright skies for the first time after what seemed months and years. And then a strange thing happens. A singular feeling comes over him of a vast and unnatural silence. He sees the mounting lark; he hears no song. It is a silent universe. Terrified, the child rushes back into the house, and there he discovers the cause of the persistent sorrow on his mother's face. He is nearly stone deaf, incurably and for ever.

His description of the fight within himself back to courage, stoicism, and acceptance of life is a very remarkable passage in the poem; and in this passage something of Treitschke's temperament throughout life is revealed. "There are men who are doomed to pass their lives on broken wings," he wrote later of Heinrich von Kleist, "because some malevolent chance has excluded them from that sphere in which alone they could accomplish the highest that is in them to do." To him in his youth that "highest" seemed his missed career of action and war. For it is certain that Treitschke, compelled to be a writer of books, would, but for this disaster, have been a soldier.

His course of study was the usual course of a young German of the time. Perhaps the greatest moment in it was when he came to the University of Bonn in 1851. There, amid the romance of the scenery, the mountains, the distant view of the spires of Köln—Balthazar, Gaspar, and Melchior, the Three Kings—the river, the castle from which Roland had started, he knew the happiest period of a university life. "He who is not a poet in Heidelberg or Bonn," he writes, "is dead to poetry." The intellectual activities of the place rapidly absorbed him. The aged poet, Moritz Arndt, was still teaching history; and one can imagine the thrill—indeed he himself has helped us to imagine it—with which the young Treitschke, with his enthusiasm for the heroes of the War of Liberation, first looked upon those high and noble features. Each successive phase of that heroic action Arndt had witnessed; his own songs had been part of the action; he had been the companion and confidant of the great minister von Stein. Even more powerful was the influence of another of the Bonn professors—Friedrich Christoph Dahlmann, the historian of Denmark. He too, like Arndt, had played his part in the War of Liberation, and at four-and-twenty he had walked across Germany with the poet of Arminius, determined to fight in the ranks of Austria, since Prussia was still too timid or too weak to strike at the tyrant. In the young student Arndt kindled memories and sentiments; but Dahlmann was at once an inspiration as a lecturer and in private a friendly adviser.

Next perhaps to the influence of Arndt and Dahlmann upon him was the influence of the Rhine. It is hard for us in England to understand what the Rhine really means to a German, the enthusiasm which he feels for that river. Treitschke himself says of it, for instance, when he has to leave Bonn: "To-morrow I shall see the Rhine for the last time. The memory of that noble river"—and this is not in a poem, observe, but simply in a letter to a friend—"the memory of that noble river will keep my heart pure and save me from sad or evil thoughts throughout all the days of my life." Try to imagine anyone saying that of the Thames!

When Treitschke becomes a teacher himself and a professor at Freiburg these are the influences governing his teaching. His own career as a teacher began at Leipzig in 1859, and he inaugurated it in a striking enough manner by his treatise on "The State." This treatise might be described as an abstract justification of monarchy, just as Rousseau's famous Essay might with fairness be described as an abstract justification of democracy. Like every sincere attempt in the field of abstract politics it is full of inconsistencies and contradictions; but it reveals the central tendencies of the author's mind. The friend of Bismarck, the apologist of the Hohenzollern and the eager admirer of Prussian bureaucracy already announces himself. The essence of the State, he argues, is power; but it is a moral power, and in virtue of this moral nature the authority of the State over the individual is supreme and without appeal.

Four years later, at Freiburg, he gave for the

first time the lectures which developed afterwards
into the two volumes entitled "Die Politik." But
the stress of the period speedily tears Treitschke
from abstract speculation upon the State to living
politics and to the study of the actions of men in
the concrete. Bismarck's struggle with the Prussian parliament is at its height. The safety and
prestige of the Prussian monarchy is not yet
assured. The dispute about the Duchies is at
hand, and behind it rises the war of 1864, and
behind the war of 1864 and the Convention of
Gastein loom the war of 1866, and Königgrätz, and
the creation of the North-German Confederation;
then the insulting half-maniacal jealousy of
France, and the war of 1870.

It is a new Germany, almost a new Europe.
Since the rise of the Spanish monarchy under
Ferdinand and Isabella and its liberation from the
Saracen dominion, and, at about the same period,
the rise of the French monarchy under Louis XI
and his successors, no event has so revolutionized
the European State-system.

Treitschke had originally been destined for the
army, and it is as a soldier of soldiers that we see
him in each phase of those momentous nine years.
"Lay on my coffin a sword," the dying Heine
wrote in 1856. But the war in which Treitschke
fought was less vague than that dim war for the
freedom of humanity in which Heine imagined
himself a fighter. Treitschke was an enthusiast

for freedom, as his essays on Milton and Byron as well as scores of passages in his other writings attest; but he plunged into the struggle to assert the Prussian ascendency over Germany with all the ardour with which, in an earlier age, Fichte and Dahlmann had plunged into the War of Liberation. At Freiburg, Kiel, and finally at Heidelberg, his own enthusiasm communicated itself to hundreds of students who heard him, and ultimately to thousands.

His appearance at this period was striking: a tall, rather slim figure, marked nobility of feature and bearing, dark eyes and masses of thick dark hair. He was sparing in gesture, abrupt and effective, more chary of pure rhetoric than Droysen, more regardful of fact than Häusser. His voice was harsh, the Saxon accent unmistakable, and he had often to pause for a word. He seldom mixed with his audience after his lectures; his deafness made this difficult, for, to a man of his sensitiveness, an ear-trumpet in general company was abhorrent. But this was no real drawback; it rather invested the speaker and his impassioned utterances with a touch of prophetic remoteness.

"Is Treitschke an orator at all?" an English admirer of his writings once asked a member of the Reichstag. "In the sense in which Mr. Gladstone was an orator," was the reply, "certainly not. In the Reichstag he is always listened to with respect; he never kindles enthusiasm; and

yet, if the art of the rhetor is to compel men to
action, how many greater orators are there in
modern Germany, or, for that matter, in modern
France or England, than simply Heinrich von
Treitschke? When I first heard him many years
ago I had been reading Palacky's History of
Bohemia. You know the book? Well, in the
thick of Ziska's tremendous duel I constantly saw
young Treitschke—for at that time he was not
more than thirty—pass between me and the page
like a Hussite warrior, authentic, irresistible, a
spiritual fatalist, like Racine's Joad girding on his
sword in the name of the Lord of Hosts. And see,
yonder he comes.''

The excitement, the momentary pallor on the
speaker's face, proved to the Englishman more
powerfully than words the dominion which intellect united to moral greatness exercises over other
men. He pointed to a solitary figure walking with
a stick slowly down the shady path of the splendid
street Unter den Linden. He walked as the deaf
always walk, glancing rapidly from side to side.
It was impossible to resist the melancholy if
penetrating strength in the dark and luminous
eyes, eyes of a type which one seldom meets in
England, full of meditative depth and integrity,
trust-winning. Once, where the crowd was less,
he raised a soft grey felt wide-awake hat, for the
day was hot, and the noble forehead was for
a second visible. Involuntarily the Englishman

raised his own hat with an instinct of reverence. That was in the summer of 1892.[1]

The years in which Treitschke wrote his greatest book are also the years of his greatest fame as a lecturer. Probably no German professor, not Fichte, not Schlosser, not Droysen, has ever commanded such audiences. His lecture-hall in Berlin did actually suggest a concourse such as, in the Middle Age, met to hear an Abelard, or, in the Renaissance time, thronged around Giordano Bruno or Pico della Mirandola.

And it was a true message, a "gospel," which they came to hear, a gospel which the commonest could understand, which the most cultured could not disdain. His subject, of course, was History, or it was Politics; but through all the mazes of historical narrative, carefully documented, fact on fact torn from hours in the Berlin archives, and amid all the mazes of political speculation, close and stern reasoning, sometimes repellent by its accumulation of apparently redundant matter and irrelevant illustration—amid all this a man's soul was wrestling almost visibly to bring home to his hearers his own burning conviction of the greatness of Germany, her past, her present, and the

[1] Treitschke's influence in the Reichstag was much greater than that of men like Lecky or Jebb or other university members in the British Parliament. It was more akin perhaps to that of John Stuart Mill when he was returned for Westminster, or to that of Macaulay.

unfathomable vistas which open out before her in the future.

That is Treitschke's central theme. It is the informing thought of each of his distinctive books or collections of writings—the five volumes of his History, the two volumes of his "Politik," his two series of "Deutsche Kämpfe, his "Bilder aus der deutschen Geschichte," his political essays and literary portraits, above all, his magnificent full-length portraits of Dahlmann and of the poet Heinrich von Kleist.

V

TREITSCHKE has no philosophy of History in the sense in which Hegel or Buckle or Cousin has a philosophy of History. He has come too late into the world for that. But in a wider sense, like every true German historian, he *has* a philosophy of History. There is nothing in which German historians more completely differ from English historians than in this respect. No German historian is ever satisfied that he has the right to teach history until he has acquired for himself by individual vision, or adopted from another, whether Kant or Hegel or Lotze or Nietzsche, some general view, some theory of the working of God in History. To him History is a drama in which God is the supreme actor. And Treitschke has such a vision or theory.

What, then, did that audience, consisting of princes and officials, of soldiers and diplomats and sometimes the most prominent figures in the Berlin fashionable world, come together to hear? They came, indeed, to hear of the greatness of Germany in other years and in other centuries. They saw pass before them in rapid sketches the grandiose or tragic forms of the Suabian and the Saxon dynasties. They were made to thrill with patriotic pride or admiration when, in speaking of a yet later age, the orator described in mordant words of contempt or denunciation the desperate conflict of France, Spain, England and Holland for exterior wealth and power, seeking a dominion upon which the sun shall never set, whilst, solitary, deep-thinking, Germany is sunk in moral and religious absorption, pursuing the freedom of the spirit, poring over the abyss of absolute ideality, founding a spiritual empire. Or the gates of Sans Souci were flung open and it was the great privilege of Treitschke's hearers to behold its builder painted with a Velasquez-like realism and a Velasquez-like sympathy, with profound imaginative insight and vision. But before all and above all that audience came together to hear the story of the manner in which God or the world-spirit, through shifting and devious paths, had led Germany and the Germans to their present exalted station under Prussia and the Hohenzollern, those great princes who in German worth and German uprightness—

Aufrichtigkeit—are unexampled in the dynasties of
Europe or of the world. Treitschke showed them
German unity, and therefore German freedom,
lying like the fragments of a broken sword, a magic
sword like that of Roland, or of Sigurd, or the
Grey-Steel of the Sagas; and these fragments
Prussia alone could weld again into dazzling
wholeness and might.

This is Treitschke's governing idea—the greatness of Prussia, the glory of an army which is a
nation and of a nation which is an army.[1]

A great Greek historian, Dion Cassius, writing
of the Roman Empire—a Greek historian, observe,
writing of the Roman Empire—said that his
conception and vision of the supreme end of
humanity was the whole world governed by the
divinely-appointed State of Rome. Similarly I
should say that this conception of the German
Fatherland, the whole German kindred, governed
by Prussia and by the House of Hohenzollern is

[1] To Giesebrecht also Germany is the nation of nations, the
people of peoples. Droysen is even more explicit. At the period
of the Schleswig-Holstein war he declared that to the Hohenzollern belonged the throne left empty or occupied by usurpers
since the death of Konradin. His "History of Prussian Policy,"
based on lectures at Jena, is governed by a similar idea. The
last volume appeared posthumously in 1886. It is a pamphlet,
and false as a pamphlet. It is impossible to read without a smile
the portraiture of the early Electors of Brandenburg as "creators
of the German idea, following, as mariners a lodestar, the conception of German unity."

the underlying theme of the Saxon Treitschke addressing a Prussian audience. And just as it had been necessary that Rome should first conquer the world in order to rule it in justice, so it had been necessary that Prussia should dominate Germany in order to give to Germany present unity and future grandeur.

When Treitschke turns from Prussia, when he turns from the War of Liberation in 1813 and casts his glance backwards across German history, that history catches fire under his pen from the power and the illumination of this same idea. The whole movement of Germany from Charlemagne, the House of Hohenstaufen, the great heroic past of the Holy Roman Empire, from the time of the Reformation and of Frederick the Great to that of Gneisenau and Stein, is towards this consummation—a united Germany under the supremacy of Prussia. And now upon what a career of high-uplifted glory shall not that mighty nation start! Once united, who shall set bounds to this Germany? What dream of the mediæval emperors, what dream of a Frederick II, "the Wonder of the World," of a Barbarossa, of an Otto I, but shall be surpassed by this Germany that he, Heinrich von Treitschke, sees arise within the frontiers of his imagination, scanning the future, brooding on things to come!

And Fate was strangely kind to Treitschke. Though dwelling in that silent universe of the

deaf, and threatened in age with the darkened
universe of the blind, he lived just long enough to
see upon the silver horizon of the North Sea, and
upon the more mysterious horizon of the Future,
the first promise of the German fleets of the
future. He saw Germany thus fitting herself for
that high task which he had marked out to one
generation after another of students—the day of
reckoning with England, the day of reckoning with
the great enemy for whom he had nevertheless that
kind of regard which every great foe inspires, which
England's strength inspires. And yet his imagination pierced beneath the semblance of her
strength, which to his imagination *was* but a
semblance.

VI

WHAT are the origins of this antagonism or this
antipathy in Treitschke to England and to things
English? The question is worth asking; for there
is no disputing Treitschke's immense influence not
only upon his own generation but upon the whole
of modern German thought.

This attitude of mind does not begin with him;
it is present in the Heidelberg School, in Häusser,
for instance, and in Schlosser; and Dahlmann's
"History of the English Revolution" is capable of
many interpretations. But in Treitschke the
antagonism reaches a height and persistence of
rancour or contempt which in so great a man is

arresting if not unique. To him the greatness of England passes with the seventeenth century, with Cromwell and Milton.

The origins of this sentiment are partly historical, partly moral, and, in Treitschke, must be sought in his character as a man and as a patriot. Britain's world-predominance outrages him as a man almost as much as it outrages him as a German. It outrages him as a man because of its immorality, its arrogance and its pretentious security. It outrages him as a German because he attributes England's success in the war for the world to Germany's preoccupation with higher and more spiritual ends. But for her absorption in those ends and the civil strife in which that absorption resulted, Germany might, in the seventeenth and eighteenth centuries, have made the Danube a German river and established a German predominance from the Bosphorus to the Indus.

The sentiment has also its roots in history, recent and remote. "France," said Bismarck in September, 1870, "must be paralyzed; for she will never forgive us our victories." And in the same spirit Treitschke avers: England will never forgive us our strength. And not without justice he delineates English policy throughout the eighteenth and nineteenth centuries as aimed consistently at the repression of Prussia, so soon as English politicians discovered the true nature of that State and divined the great future reserved for it by destiny. Had not England been Prussia's treacherous but timid enemy in 1864 and 1866, and again in 1870–71, and, above all, in 1874–75?

But the strongest motive is the conviction, which becomes more intense as the years advance, that Britain's world-predominance is out of all proportion to Britain's real strength and to her worth or value, whether that worth be considered in the political, the social, the intellectual, or the moral sphere. It is the detestation of a sham. "In this universe of ours the thing that is wholly a sham—wholly rotten—may endure for a time, but cannot endure for ever." This is the protest of the stern apostle of reality. He frequently rings the changes on the "nation of shopkeepers," pointing with aptness and justice to the general meanness and gradually increasing sordidness of English political life. That which Treitschke hates in England is what Napoleon hated in England—a pretentiousness, an overweening middle-class self-satisfaction, which is not really patriotism, not the high and serious passion of Germany in 1813 and 1870, but an insular narrow conceit; in fact, the emotion enshrined in that most vulgar of all national hymns, "Rule Britannia"!

> "The nations not so blest as thee
>   Must in their turn to tyrants fall,
>   Whilst thou shalt flourish, great and free
>   The dread and envy of them all."

Consider the world-picture which that upcalls! A single island usurping the glory of freedom, surrounded by a world groaning beneath tyrants, whilst she sits in lonely grandeur!

For Treitschke it is not genius, it is not valour, it is not even great policy, as in the case of Venice, which has built up the British Empire; but the hazard of her geographical situation, the supineness of other nations, the measureless duplicity of her ministers, and the natural and innate hypocrisy of the nation as a whole. These have let this monstrous empire grow—a colossus with feet of clay. Along with this he has the conviction that such a power can be overthrown. And with what a stern joy and self-congratulation would not the nations acclaim the destruction of the island-State, "Old England," old, indeed, and corrupt, rotten through and through!

The sincerity as well as the intensity of Treitschke's anti-Englishism is attested by the spontaneity and variety with which it finds expression. The indignation of Schlosser, judging his contemporaries as Dante judged his contemporaries, is a dispersed indignation; Treitschke's is concentrated upon England only. His inventiveness is astonishing. Here he takes up a phrase of Montesquieu, who in "The Spirit of Laws" makes England, so to speak, the hero of that great and perfect book, and he turns Montesquieu's judgment into an occasion for a diatribe not only against French character in the eighteenth century, but against the whole character of English history. At another time he attacks the private character of the English in a manner that recalls Nietzsche's witty apophthegm, when, speaking of the part played by danger and suffering in the heroic life, he observes, "Man, after all, does not really desire happiness; only the Englishman does that," thus adroitly placing the Englishman outside the pale of humanity altogether. But Treitschke is seldom witty, though often grossly if unintentionally offensive. He is as unable as Heine to see anything fine in the English character.

"Foreign critics do not like my books? That is natural. I write for Germans, not foreigners," he answered with impatient contempt when an admirer pointed out to him the injury he did to his chances of a European success like that of Ranke or Mommsen. And in the love and measureless admiration of his own nation he has had his reward.

One final question. When, by the light of what is called "impartial history,"[1] one considers the events of the last century in their bearing on Treitschke's theory of Germany's future, whither does Germany in that century, at once in politics

[1] Of course there is no such thing as "impartial history," and even if there could be impartial history it would be the dullest, stupidest thing on this earth of ours.

and in thought, really seem to be moving? In the first place, if we contrast the Germany of the present day with the old half-idyllic, half-despotic Germany of Goethe's great youth and early fame,[1] of Lessing's manhood, of Schiller's early years, of Herder and the Jacobis—that Germany, almost patriarchal in its simplicity, quite clearly has passed away for ever. Its exclusive ideal was culture, not patriotism, and the first word in culture always is Mankind, *Humanitas*, Humanity. It was essentially, that is to say, a cosmopolitan Germany. Goethe, for instance, when his whole nation, convulsed by the war against Napoleon, is looking to him for guidance—how does the great poet of Germany act? He turns aside altogether from the present and resolutely fixes his imagination upon Persia! Upon Persian poetry, the Persian Divans, the beauties of Jallal'ud'din, of Ḥafiz, of Sa'di! And in regard to Napoleon he said to a German friend, "That fellow is far too strong for you; you'll never do anything against him." But men can now no longer say with Jacobi, "I hear on every side nowadays the word 'German,' but who is a German? I strive in vain as yet to attach any precise meaning to the term"; or with Lessing himself that patriotism is nothing but an heroic weakness that he for one is glad to be

[1] That is to say, the period in which he writes "Werther," the First Part of "Wilhelm Meister," and the First Part of "Faust," and those great dramas "Iphigenie" and "Tasso."

rid of; or with Herder, "Of all kinds of pride I hold national pride the most foolish; it ruined Greece; it ruined Judæa and Rome." Gone, too, are the days of Karl Immermann, who could never follow a political debate because he could form no image of such abstractions.[1]

There you have that earlier, and, if you choose to call it so, that greater Germany. But what Treitschke sees underneath that is the Germany of the War of Liberation, Prussia renascent, and her steady advance throughout the nineteenth century to the present day. And as Treitschke, casting his eyes back to primitive German history, sees arise there the religion of the valiant, the religion of Valour, so now, with this informing thought in the mind, we can trace in the Germany of 1913 like a dawn upon the horizon, piercing like a sun through all the transient mists of industrialism, socialism, militarism, the vision of that same religion returning to Germany—that Religion of Valour.

[1] That was the Germany very largely of Hegel; it certainly was the Germany of Kant. And to him also, I daresay, though we have no record of it, it would have been difficult to associate, there at Königsberg, any particular meaning with the words "German patriotism."

LECTURE IV

I

IN speaking the concluding words on a great subject the endeavour to choose from among the multitude of ideas which throng in upon the mind discourages the imagination, oppressing it with a sense of the inadequacy, if not the uselessness, of any effort to pierce the future or to trace its probable course in the history of two nations. How is it possible to discover any principle which will enable us to conjecture, even in outline, the future of two such empires as Germany and England?

I remember that narrative in Ordericus of the death-bed of one of our greatest kings, one of the most heroic and tragic figures of modern history. Dying, he augured of the future; he saw disaster descending upon his own work and upon this nation; he augured of the conduct and careers of individuals. The irony in a Greek tragedy, in which Destiny seems to take a clear joy in making sport of the anticipations and desires of men, is not more scornful than the irony with which Destiny turned to nothingness the auguries of the dying Norman, alike in regard to individuals and to nations.

The temptation therefore is to be silent, to avoid any prophecy whatever, to say bluntly and at once, "The future is impenetrable," or again, "It is inevitable as the past"—equally inevitable whether we regard the bloody strivings of this universe as blind chance or as the eternal unwinding and winding of a predetermined or arbitrary scheme.

Yet History itself becomes mere picturesque anecdote as in Macaulay, or an unending series of brilliant biographies as in Carlyle, or a staid reconstruction of Council or Parliamentary procedure as in Hallam and Stubbs, unless, after a long sojourn in the past and a steady gaze into the future out of the past, the present becomes, as it were, transparent and the forms of the future, dim and colossal like clouds or the dark procession of trees reflected in water, become obscurely visible. Unless the study of the past of two such nations as Germany and England, nations which some fifteen hundred years ago lived side by side within their native woods, enables one to form some perception, to attain to some *Ahnung*, as a German would say, of the inward fate which shapes the destiny of nations, History itself in any true sense becomes impossible.

In support of this principle I may point out that between the lives of nations and of individual men there is, after all, another distinction than that of longevity. The final test is not arithmetic; for whilst he who ventures to vaticinate on the career of an individual, to generalize upon its future course from temperament or from strength of purpose, may in an instant be derided by some of the myriad forms which "Chance" assumes—a sudden illness, a street accident, some untoward occurrence from the past, the action of a friend or enemy—he who deals with the careers of nations and peoples is secure from such misadventures. In the life of a nation "accident," or "Chance," the dread mistress of accident, plays a part so slight that it can all but be ignored. It is this, therefore, which subordinates the history of nations to law and to cause and effect rather than, as in the individual life, to accident. The power of cause and effect, however commonly it may be talked of, is, in the individual life, a minimum. Many years ago Schopenhauer pointed out the force of this contrast. War, indeed, seems to expose a nation to fortune; yet Russia is already recovering from the campaign in Manchuria, Mukden is forgotten, and Russia has resumed her resistless path, slow as the movement of a glacier but as sure.

And there is another respect in which the destiny of nations differs from the destiny of men. In the conscious action of individuals motive or purpose is supreme; but the forces which govern the action of States approximate more closely to the operation of causes in the natural world. They can more readily be grouped under laws. A science of politics thus becomes possible; a philosophy of history a pursuit. Religion is the very essence of both; history becomes religion, religion history; for ultimately the supreme Actor in history and in politics is God. Time's drama, world rising behind world, universe behind universe, is His drama; its theatre this far-outspanned fabric of star-drift and suns, of fire-cloud and sunk system blackening in ether; and here, on this planet, great nations, cities and empires are the brief embodiments or the transient realizations of His desires. Thus the nearer man's portraiture of God approaches to reality the nearer will his philosophy of history approach to a complete harmony between semblance and substance, that is, towards Truth. For History, the course of events, is not the light, but, as its name, ἱστορία implies, a continuous searching for the light—the world-spirit down the ages seeking the realization of its ultimate desire, a tragic realization because it can only end in the destruction of the world-soul's Being as such.

Regarding this universe and man's history, then, as a movement towards a fixed end and a tragic end, how shall one determine the sphere or define the operation of cause and of law in the history of nations? For just as from the motion of a planet

causes, say, of the French Revolution, or the Hundred Years' War against France, or the fall of Rome or of Venice. Only a year ago, in speaking of the causes of the French Revolution, I pointed out how superficial is that view of the French Revolution which attributes it only to the writings of Voltaire and of Rousseau. How common is that explanation! Yet if you universalize this seeming cause of the French Revolution that too evaporates.

But if true causes in history are difficult to discover, it does not follow that they are undiscoverable, or that, in our effort to attain to a perception of the deep underlying forces in the inward fate and destiny of nations, some true cause may not disclose itself and make the gauging, the measuring, the computing with regard to the future, something more than mere conjecture; and it is this which renders it possible to deal with our subject here to-day.

II

IN the present and future relations of England and Germany is it, then, possible out of the past to discover the operation of such forces or causes as will enable us to conjecture the future rôles of these two nations?

First of all, it is evident that the region in which one must seek them is the region in which England's needs come most sharply into conflict with

Germany's desires. And here a law, obvious, universal and inevitable in its application, discloses itself. It concerns the struggle for power. Amongst free independent nations weakness means war; and the empire which is not prepared to defend itself by forces proportionate to the magnitude of that empire must fall.

The period at which an empire becomes stationary can never be more than approximately determined. Thus in the history of Rome it may be assigned to the sixty years between the accession of Hadrian and the death of Marcus Aurelius; and in that of Venice to the fifty years between the dogeship of Antonio Grimani and that of Luigi Mocenigo. But in each case that period also announces the beginning of the decline; for here again nations are subject to the operations of natural law, and it may be affirmed that the empire which has ceased to advance has begun to recede and therefore to decline, and the empire which has begun to decline is dead already.

There comes, for instance, a moment in the history of Rome when the question of putting an end to Rome's attempt to govern the whole world is repeatedly before Roman thinkers and politicians. And from the first century of the Roman era men recalled a strange circumstance. When the city was founded the assembled gods each gave to Rome some beneficence, some great faculty peculiar to himself; but Terminus, the god of

Boundaries, of Limitations, on that memorable day refused his gift, defying even the master of the gods, Jupiter himself. And the Roman augurers took this as a symbol that in the future there should be no boundaries set to Rome's dominion, that there never would come a time when she should abandon her world-mission. In the reign of Hadrian, however, there came at last a moment when a term was set to Rome's advance, when, from jealousy of his predecessor Trajan, Hadrian gave back the former's Eastern conquests and withdrew within the earlier limits of the empire. And the wits of Rome then said that the god Terminus, who had defied Jupiter, had yielded most courteously to the Emperor Hadrian!

Has such a moment come for England? Is there any reason why we should now tolerate the courtesy of the god Terminus? Is there a limit to our expansion? Until the last decade of the nineteenth century the history of Imperial Britain is one of rapid and easy advance, in the Mediterranean, in the Atlantic, in the Southern Seas, amongst the Pacific Isles. Did she reach in that decade that stage when an empire, ceasing to advance, has begun to recede and therefore to decline? And was the Boer War a proof at once of her weakness and her strength? This is the real problem of imperialism in 1913.

In contrast to this, what of Germany? I have described the attitude of the youth of Germany, soldiers, students, professors, politicians, writers of books. Their position is clear. "Are we to acquiesce," they ask, "in England's possession of one-fifth of the globe, with no title-deeds, no claim, except priority in robbery? Our greatest teachers so describe it." And I showed you how young Germans of the twentieth century can, in support of this position, appeal to the representations of English history by many of the most commanding intellects of their own nation, expressed in guarded or unguarded terms. They can even cite the Englishman Seeley as a witness to the dominion which hazard has played in England's uncouth and unmerited grandeur. She is the Malvolio of nations; greatness has been thrust upon her.

And then follows the fixed and inevitable conclusion, now silent but deeply and passionately resentful, now clamorous and aggressive, as in the Prussian war-party and its adherents in every rank of Prussian life: "Is all indeed lost; and is the war for the world ended? In the world-arena has Germany, like a belated champion, girt in her shining armour, ridden up to the great tourney too late? Has Destiny, like a herald, by a trumpet's sound proclaimed the lists closed? Must the splintered sword which Germany has at last succeeded in welding into a solid blade so dazzling and terrific—must it indeed rest in its sheath for ever? Can the youth of Germany acquiesce in this cowardly renunciation and not forfeit honour and, with honour, manhood?" Hence the real force and the real meaning of Bernhardi's iterated watchword: "Empire or Downfall—*Weltmacht oder Niedergang.*" It is as if he said: "World-dominion or Death."

Such then is the situation and such are the problems which in the immediate future confront all that is young, all that is ardent throughout Germany, in those teeming cities and towns, those universities and gymnasia. Every decade, every half decade leaves the question more poignant. With every advance in her conscious strength which the Germany of Wilhelm II makes on land or in the air or on the sea the necessity of an answer will become more imperious, the terms of the problem more strict and confined, and, other things remaining the same, the resultant rancour of mind more feverish.[1]

---

[1] Other contingencies than war with England are possible in the immediate future. A war with France, as a military critic insists, may break out at any moment, and, assuming that England stands cynically aloof, that war, if France is permitted to work out her three-years system, may end in a drawn game, though by its savage fury leaving both nations so weak from hæmorrhage that a quarter of a century will be necessary for either to recover its prestige. On the other hand, Germany may decide not to await the development of the three-years system in France, and, trusting to diplomats and to her present enormous superiority in numbers, may strike France without a declaration of war and overwhelm her by sheer weight.

This is Bernhardi's interpretation of Germany's duty, for it would leave Germany front to front with England. France

III

Now let me examine the subject more from the standpoint of history than that of politics. Burke long since deprecated the drawing up of an indictment against a whole nation, and Sir Thomas Browne in a famous passage has stigmatized "the sin against charity" involved in all such indictments. It is scarcely less hazardous or less difficult to characterize with sureness the temper or the mood of a people in this or that period of its history. And yet when such familiarity as leisure affords and unbiased inquiry, anxious only to see the thing as in very deed it is[1] and as in very deed it has arisen, leave a definite impression on the mind, it can hardly be a "sin against charity"

---

humiliated, the incorporation, on advantageous terms, of Holland with the German Empire would be easy. The submission or annexation of Belgium would follow of itself.

With regard to the enmity between Russia and Germany, in Germany's antagonism to Russia there is nothing fateful, nothing organic. It is a wound that, as Bismarck once very profoundly said, can be cauterized at any moment, because there is not and never has been any innate cause for war between Germany and Russia. Germany does not seek Constantinople; her patronage of Turkey was the natural reply to the unnatural alliance of France and Russia. But the enmity of England and Germany is like one of those springs that rise from the nether deep; the more you try to fill them up the wider they become.

[1] To me the most disquieting thing in our relations to Germany is our politicians' fixed resolution to see things *other* than as they are.

or render me subject to the accusation of rashness if I state that impression.

Already the minds which determine the action of nations, touched with the lure of world-dominion, compare the resolution and emotion which this vision of Germany's future stirs in its devotees to the emotion and great resolve of Faust, when, conquering his past and freed from his remorses, he wakens amid the glittering solitudes of the Alps, sees the sun above the summits, sees the rainbow span the cataract, and speaks the noble verses:

"Du, Erde, wanst auch diese Nacht beständig
. Und atmest neu erquickt zu meinen Füssen,
Beginnest schon mit Lust mich zu umgeben.
Du regst und rührst ein kräftiges Beschliessen,
Zum höchsten Dasein immerfort zu streben."[1]

But what, it may be asked, is that highest being, that highest ideal? It is world-dominion; it is world-empire; it is the hegemony of a planet. It assigns to Germany in the future a rôle like that which Rome or Hellas or Judæa or Islâm have played in the past. That is Germany's hero-ideal. It is at least greatly conceived.

[1] "Thou, Earth, this night wast also constant found,
And breathest, newly quickened, at my feet,
Already with delight encircling me.
Thou wak'st and stir'st in me a strong resolve—
Towards highest being onwards still to strive."

Assuming for a moment that this world-predominance is possible to Germany, what is the testimony of Germany's past to her capacity to play this rôle?   You find Germany an empire already in the seventh century, if you regard Charlemagne as a German—as he was; and again you have attempts at imperialism made by the German race under the Ottos in the tenth century; but most distinctly is Germany an imperial power in the twelfth century, in the time of the Hohenstaufen, one of the most tragic dynasties in history. She then has Italy as her appanage; and her record there, under Frederick I, Henry VI, and Frederick II, is the record in Ireland of England at her worst.

Again, the history of Germany as an imperial power in the seventeenth and eighteenth centuries centres in the records of the Habsburgs in Italy; and it is impossible not to observe that the presence of the Habsburgs, of the Germans, as an imperial power in Italy, is synchronous with the defeat and obliteration of Italian art, Italian literature, Italian religion, and Italian patriotism.   And in the nineteenth century Germany's power in Italy centres in the name of Metternich, that minister who stands in the annals of European history as the synonym of reaction and oppression, the man who employed the dungeon and the fortress as the chief instruments of an enlightened government!

Here, then, is the augury that the past affords

as to the future of Germany as a world-civilizing power.   Here we have the record of the *past*—I stress the word.

But, it is argued, this is not the true Germany. Those attempts under the Ottos in the tenth century, and in the twelfth and thirteenth under the great House of Hohenstaufen, are attempts at empire indeed, but the German nation as such takes no part in them.   German imperialism in that period is, as it were, forced upon it from without.   The nation is indifferent to empire. The true impulse of the people is to be found in the Free Cities, for instance in the Hansa League. And the passing away of those early efforts is succeeded by a period of purely dynastic efforts at empire in Germany, in which the nation becomes divorced entirely from the action of the governing House, the House of Habsburg.   So that, until the present time, until, as Treitschke admirably points out, the Hohenzollern became the paramount power in Germany, there has been no national attempt at empire at all.   The true German genius, Treitschke himself affirms, only finds its expression under the domination of Prussia and of the Hohenzollern.   The beginnings of German imperialism, that is to say, are to be found only in the Germany of the last hundred years under that glorious House!

Germany's *past* as a world-civilizing power does not concern the German thinkers of to-day.

"We give the past," they say, "to England. When we speak of empire the empire we mean is in the future. You have drunk the wine of empire. It is Germany's turn now. And it is vain to look back to the Hohenstaufen and to the Habsburgs in Italy. Just as it would be vain to appeal to England's conduct in Ireland in the fourteenth and fifteenth centuries for the augury of England's conduct as an empire in India under Cornwallis and Wellesley, Dalhousie and Canning, so it is vain to appeal to the past of Germany in Italy for any augury of the character of the empire that shall arise in the future out of Germany."

Treitschke has defined the aim of Germany, and Treitschke's definition, which has been taken up by his disciples, is this: That just as the greatness of Germany is to be found in the governance of Germany by Prussia, so the greatness and good of the world is to be found in the predominance there of German culture, of the German mind—in a word, of the German character. This is the ideal of Germany, and this is Germany's rôle as Treitschke saw it in the future.

For, observe, this world-dominion of which Germany dreams is not simply a material dominion. Germany is not blind to the lessons inculcated by the Napoleonic tyranny. Force alone, violence or brute strength, by its mere silent presence or by its loud manifestation in war, may be necessary to establish this dominion;

but its ends are spiritual. The triumph of the Empire will be the triumph of German culture, of the German world-vision in all the phases and departments of human life and energy, in religion, poetry, science, art, politics, and social endeavour.

The characteristics of this German world-vision, the benefits which its predominance is likely to confer upon mankind, are, a German would allege, truth instead of falsehood in the deepest and gravest preoccupations of the human mind; German sincerity instead of British hypocrisy; Faust instead of Tartuffe. And whenever I have put to any of the adherents of this ideal the further question: "Where in actual German history do you find your guarantee for the character of this spiritual empire; is not the true rôle of Germany cosmopolitan and peaceful; are not Herder and Goethe its prophets?" I have met with one invariable answer: "The political history of Germany, from the accession of Frederick in 1740 to the present hour, has admittedly no meaning unless it be regarded as a movement towards the establishment of a world-empire, with the war against England as the necessary preliminary. Similarly the curve which, during the last century and a half, Germany has traced in religion and metaphysical thought, from Kant and Hegel to Schopenhauer, Strauss, and Nietzsche, has not less visibly been a movement towards a newer world-religion, a newer world-faith. That fatal tendency to cosmopolitanism, to a dream-world, which Heine derided[1] and Treitschke deplores, does, indeed, still remain, but how transfigured!"

But what definitely is to be Germany's part in the future of human thought? Germany answers: "It is reserved for us to resume in thought that creative rôle in religion which the whole Teutonic race abandoned fourteen centuries ago. Judæa and Galilee cast their dreary spell over Greece and Rome when Greece and Rome were already sinking into decrepitude and the creative power in them was exhausted, when weariness and bitterness wakened with their greatest spirits at day and sank to sleep again with them at night. But Judæa and Galilee struck Germany in the splendour and heroism of her prime. Germany and the whole Teutonic people in the fifth century made the great error. They conquered Rome, but, dazzled by Rome's authority, they adopted the religion and the culture of the vanquished. Germany's own deep religious instinct, her native genius for religion, manifested in her creative success,[2] was arrested, stunted, thwarted. But,

---

[1] "Sohn der Thorheit! träume immer,
    Wenn dirs Herz im Busen schwillt;
    Doch im Leben suche nimmer
    Deines Traumes Ebenbild!"

                (Werke, Elster's ed., vol. ii., p. 159.)

[2] Gothic architecture, the abbeys and cathedrals from Burgos to Chartres and Köln, are the living witnesses to the Teuton's imagination in the new religion.

having once adopted the new faith, she strove to live that faith, and for more than thirty generations she has struggled and wrestled to see with eyes that were not her eyes, to worship a God that was not her God, to live with a world-vision that was not her vision, and to strive for a heaven that was not her heaven. And with what chivalry and with what loyalty did not Germany strive! With what ardour she flung herself first into the pursuit of sainthood as an ideal and then into the Crusades! Conrad and Barbarossa, Otto the Great and Frederick II, Hildebrand and Innocent III, were of her blood, so were Godfrey and Tancred and Bohemund. Yet in the East, in the very height of her enthusiasm, the outward fabric of faith sank. In the East where she sought the grave of Christ she saw beyond it the grave of Balder, and higher than the New Jerusalem the shining walls of Asgard and of Valhalla. In Jerusalem, standing beside an empty grave, the summits of a mightier vision gleamed spectral around her. And whilst her Crusaders, front to front with Islâm, burst into passionate denials and set Mohammed above Christ, or in exasperated scorn derided all religion, her great thinkers and mystics led her steadily toward the serener heights where knowledge and faith dissolve in vision, and ardour is all.

"A great hope had sunk; a mightier hope had arisen. But, like the purposes of the world-spirit in everlasting self-disaccord, this hope could only be born in the bloodiest strife, and agony infinite, and fertilizing hatred and war. This is the true import of that long conflict which begins with the Schmalkaldic League and only ends on the battlefields of Tilly and Wallenstein, Gustavus Adolphus, Bernhard of Saxe Weimar and Torstensen. Rome no longer a guide, Germany was torn by the violence of furious heresies, from which sprang the wild secret orgies of the Black Mass, and that subterranean literature of which the 'De Tribus Impostoribus' is a sign.

"The seventeenth century flung off Rome; the eighteenth undermined Galilee itself; Strauss completed the task that Eichhorn began; and with the opening of the twentieth century, Germany, her long travail past, is re-united to her pristine genius, her creative power in religion and in thought.

"And what is the religion which, on the whole, may be characterized as the religion of the most earnest and passionate minds of young Germany? What is this new movement? The movement, the governing idea of the centuries from the fourteenth to the nineteenth, is the wrestle of the German intellect not only against Rome, but against Christianism itself. Must Germany submit to this alien creed derived from an alien clime? Must she for ever confront the ages the borrower of her religion, her own genius for religion numbed and paralyzed?

"Hence the significance of Nietzsche. Kant compromises, timid and old; Hegel finds the Absolute Religion in Christianity; Schopenhauer turns to the East and at thirty-one adapts the Upanishads to the Western mind; David Friedrich Strauss, whilst denying and rejecting the metaphysic of Christianity, clings to the ethics. But Nietzsche? Nietzsche clears away the 'accumulated rubbish' of twelve hundred years; he attempts to set the German imagination back where it was with Alaric and Theodoric, fortified by the experience of twelve centuries to confront the darkness unaided, unappalled, triumphant, great and free.

"Thus, while preparing to found a world-empire, Germany is also preparing to create a world-religion. No cultured European nation since the French Revolution has made any experiment in creative religion. The experiment which England, with her dull imagination, has recoiled from, Germany will make; the fated task which England has declined, she will essay."

That is the faith of young Germany in 1913. The prevalent bent of mind at the universities, in the army amongst the more cultured, is towards what may be described as the religion of Valour, reinterpreted by Napoleon and by Nietzsche— the glory of action, heroism, the doing of great things. It is in metaphysics Zarathustra's "Amor Fati." It is in politics and ethics Napoleonism.

These same young men, who, in this very month, thrill with the scenes of 1813, see in Napoleon the oppressor, but they see in Napoleon's creed the springs of his action, a message of fire: Live dangerously!

Kant's great Imperative was born of the defeats and of the victories of Frederick; echoes from Kolin and Kunersdorf, as well as from Rossbach, thrid along its majestic phrasing; it is moulded in heroic suffering and brought forth in resignation and in grief that is overcome. But in the newer Imperative ring the accents of an earlier, greater prime, the accents heard by the Scamander, which even at Chaeronea did not entirely die away:

"Ye have heard how in old times it was said, Blessed are the meek, for they shall inherit the earth; but I say unto you, Blessed are the valiant, for they shall make the earth their throne. And ye have heard men say, Blessed are the poor in spirit; but I say unto you, Blessed are the great in soul and the free in spirit, for they shall enter into Valhalla. And ye have heard men say, Blessed are the peacemakers; but I say unto you, Blessed are the war-makers, for they shall be called, if not the children of Jahve, the children of Odin, who is greater than Jahve."

IV

THE influence which Napoleon exercises upon modern German thought is peculiar and instructive. In Europe as a whole, in the twentieth century, two great spirit-forces contend for men's allegiance—Napoleon and Christ. The one, the representative of life-renunciation, places the reconciliation of life's discords and the solution of its problems in a tranquil but nebulous region beyond the grave; the other, the asserter of earth and of earth's glories, disregardful of any life beyond the grave, finds life's supreme end in heroism and the doing of great things, and seeks no immortality except the immortality of renown, and even of that he is slightly contemptuous. To Napoleon the end of life is power and the imposing of his will upon the wills of other men. Like Achilles or like Ajax, ever to be the first and to outshine all others is his confessed ambition. The law, on the other hand, which Christ laid upon men appears to be the law of self-effacement. The true Christist toils but for others; he prays but for others. He suffers for them; he dies for them; *Servus servorum Dei*—slave of the slaves of God—was the proud subscription which the haughtiest of the mediæval Pontiffs placed at the end of their letters.

In Europe, I say, this conflict between Christ and Napoleon for the mastery over the minds of men is the most significant spiritual phenomenon of the twentieth century. You meet with it in England and in America, as in Austria and Spain. You meet with it even in Italy. In Russia Tolstoi's furious attacks are a proof of its increasing sway. The new spirit in France is its unacknowledged derivative. But it is in Germany alone that as yet Napoleonism has acquired something of the clearness and self-consistency of a formulated creed, above all in Berlin and in the cities and towns that come most within the influence of Berlin. They have not forgotten 1806 and the years of hideous humiliation which followed; they have not forgotten the German conscripts who were compelled to fight under the banners of their conqueror; they have not forgotten the 297,000 men of German blood, who under the Corsican's leadership, had, in 1812, to march against Russia; nor have they forgotten 1813 and the tremulous awful hour when the destinies of Europe and, so to speak, of the world, hung in the balance at Dresden, at Kulm, at Katzbach and at Leipzig. But, whilst abjuring the tyrant of Germany and the oppressor of Europe, they have gradually acquired a profound and ever profounder reverence for the creed and the religion towards which that great and solitary spirit, perhaps the loneliest amongst the children of men, still struggled amid the tumults and desolations, the triumphs and the glories, the victory and the disaster of his tragic and brief career—a world-tragedy, his, at once the Man of Destiny and the Antagonist of Destiny.

More than the Europe of 1800 and 1801, which

saw in the victor of Marengo the Mohammed of a
new era, the enunciator of a new faith, young Germany, the Germany of to-day, in the writings of
Treitschke and of the followers of Treitschke,
studies Napoleonism, illumining politics with an
austere and uplifting grandeur. In the writings of
Nietzsche and of the followers of Nietzsche they
study the same Napoleonism transforming the
principles of everyday life, breathing a new
spirit into ethics, transfiguring the tedious, half-
hypocritical morality of an earlier generation.
Remorse for the great error of the race in the fifth
century has ousted every other admiration.

Corsica, in a word, has conquered Galilee.

And the future? All there is as yet obscure; but
that "empire of the spirit" will certainly be something of wider range, of indefinitely wider range
than the whole of the confederated German world,
or any idealization of that world, however up-
lifted or sublime. One mighty issue is secured:
Germany at least shall not confront the twentieth
century and its thronging vicissitudes as the
worshipper of an alien God, thrall of an alien
morality. Dazzling as Elpore[1] with the dawn-star
above her brow, the New Germany, knit once
more to the divine genius within herself, delivered
from the loathed burden of the past, the cancer of
the centuries, confronts the vast darkness.

The rôle of a new Judæa or a new Hellas is lofty

[1] See Goethe's " *Pandora*."

enough to stimulate the imagination and give an inspiration to the monotony of contemporary life. But this changed and changing Europe of ours, this changed and changing world, does it definitely forbid or nobly encourage that hope? Do the present conditions of the world permit of a new Judæa or a new Hellas?

History, I have somewhere said, never really repeats itself—except in the leading articles of newspapers! But in the years in front, ineffectively and impotently crowded by Nietzsche with his ambiguous caricature, the Superman, a thing made by Nature's journeyman—in that future what newer path to a newer world-vision, what creative, all-informing, all-comprehensive thought which shall extort a reluctant homage even from the East, may not the German imagination, its fetters broken, now carve? Till now all has been negative. Chaos has returned; but out of that chaos what new and miraculous cosmos may not the German imagination raise?

That world-empire of which Germany dreams she may, or may not, on its material side, attain; but in this race for the spirit's dominion, the mightier empire of human Thought, who is her rival? Where even is her competitor? Not England assuredly; for in that region England in the twentieth century has a place retrograde almost as Austria or Spain; not America; not Russia; not Japan, with her tasteless, over-eager

efforts to enter the comity of Europe. Is it
France? . . .

*　　*　　*　　*　　*

[*The discussion of this question was here broken off as
the lecture hour was nearing its end; and it is not
possible to fill the gap from any notes left by the
lecturer. The "ambitions" spoken of in the first
sentence of Section V are clearly those of world-
empire "on its material side."*]

V

If these, then, are the legitimate impulses, the just
ambitions of Germany—and what Englishman
remembering the methods by which the British
Empire has been established in India, in America,
in Africa, in Egypt, dare arraign those impulses or
those ambitions?—if these are the modes which the
"will to power" assumes in modern Germany,
what of England and those needs of England with
which they enter most immediately into collision?

And here it is necessary, as a preliminary, to
consider the purpose of British Imperialism at the
present day and the manner in which that purpose
has been evolved; to consider what the past of
England and of this empire of ours has been, what
has been the ideal shaped in that past and what it is
that has made the greatness of England.

Now assuredly there was never a period in our
history when it was more essential than at the pres-

ent that every Englishman should have some clear
conception of what the words "Empire" and
"Imperialism" really mean, what they have
meant in the past. Yet there has never been a
period in which those words were employed more
vaguely or more variously; and vague words lead
to vague actions. England in the twentieth
century has reached that transition stage in the
history of all empires when more or less unconscious effort passes into conscious realization and
achievement. We are passing, that is to say, from
the period when we created this empire almost
without knowing it, to a period in which all the
latent purposes of our history have emerged into
the full survey of everyday criticism, everyday comment. This consciousness or over-consciousness
of empire is a new phase in the political life of
England and is of momentous significance. The
mind of the race, absorbed no longer in the onward
striving, dwells persistently, at times morbidly, on
its present greatness, or, turning backward, re-
interprets the past by the light of the present, and
in nearer or remoter actions and eras discovers
purposes which were unsuspected alike by the
heroes of those actions and by their contemporaries, but which led inevitably to the present.

In Roman history the age of Augustus offers the
most exact analogy to the twentieth century in the
history of Imperial Britain. Montesquieu, survey-
ing the work of the early kings of Rome, clinches

the survey in the fine and telling phrase: "They had already begun to build the eternal city." But even Livy, writing his History under the dominion of a single thought, is too much of an historian, amid all his rhetoric, to ascribe to any Roman politician or to any Roman orator before the time of Sulla so terse and conscious an interpretation of Rome's mission as that which Virgil has placed in the mouth of Anchises:

"Excudent alii spirantia mollius æra,
   credo equidem, vivos ducent de marmore vultus,
   orabunt causas melius, cœlique meatus
   describent radio et surgentia sidera dicent:
   tu regere imperio populos, Romane, memento;
   hæ tibi erunt artes; pacisque imponere morem,
   parcere subjectis et debellare superbos."[1]

There are other points of resemblance. Britain's concession of practical autonomy to South Africa, before the traces of war had vanished from farm and veldt, extorted the admiration of Europe; but it has its parallel on an even greater scale in Cæsar's grant of the franchise to the Gauls and in his formation of the Gaulic legions.

[1] "Others, I know it well, the breathing bronze shall chase,
   And from the death-cold marble upcall the living face,
   Shall plead with eloquence not thine, shall mete and map the skies,
   And with the voice of science tell when stars shall set and rise:
   Be thine, O Rome, to rule; nor e'er this destiny forgo,
   To spare who yield submission, and bring the haughty low."

Is it possible, then, at such a transition period as the present, which, just because it *is* a transition period, is therefore as dangerous to a nation as is a flank-march to an army—is it possible to form any clear conception of what "Empire" has really always meant to England, whether in extreme consciousness or in the dark unconscious? Can one define with any precision the aims which British Imperialism has unconsciously pursued in the past, and the ends which it more or less consciously pursues in the present?

Let me illustrate my answer by an incident from Greek history.[1] On the night before Alexander of Macedon started for the East on that career of conquest in which, like Achilles, his great exemplar, he was to find his glory and an early death, he had a farewell interview with the man who had been his tutor, now the master of a rising school of thought in the shades of the Lyceum. And towards the close of the interview Aristotle said to the Macedonian:

"You are about to start upon an enterprise which will bring you into many lands and amongst many nations, some already celebrated in arts and arms, some savage and unknown. But this last counsel I give you: Whithersoever your victories

[1] [NOTE.—*The authority for this incident in its present form cannot be traced; but as Professor Cramb used it both in his writings and lectures it is probable that, in his exceptionally wide studies in classical literature, he had come across it in some little-known author.*]

lead you, never forget that you are a Greek, and everywhere draw hard and fast the line that separates the Greek from the Barbarian."

"No," answered the youthful conqueror—he was barely two-and-twenty—"I will pursue another policy. I will make all men Hellenes. That shall be the purpose of my victories."

The wisdom of a soldier for once went deeper than the wisdom of the greatest architect of thought that Time has known.

And two centuries later a Greek writer gave definiteness to the Macedonian's reply when he described the influence of the Greek spirit under the Roman dominion as tending to give all men a Greek mind, to give all men the power to look at man's life, man's actions, man's past and future, from the standpoint of the Greek.

In the same manner, if I were asked how one could describe in a sentence the general aim of British Imperialism during the last two centuries and a half, I should answer in the spirit of Dionysius: To give all men within its bounds an English mind; to give all who come within its sway the power to look at the things of man's life, at the past, at the future, from the standpoint of an Englishman; to diffuse within its bounds that high tolerance in religion which has marked this empire from its foundation; that reverence yet boldness before the mysteriousness of life and death, characteristic of our great poets and our great thinkers; that love of free institutions, that pursuit of an ever-higher justice and a larger freedom which, rightly or wrongly, we associate with the temper and character of our race wherever it is dominant and secure.[1]

That is the conception of Empire and of England which persists through the changing fortunes of parties and the rise and fall of Cabinets. It outlives the generations. Like an immortal energy it links age to age. This undying spirit is the true England, the true Britain, for which men strive and suffer in every zone and in every era, which silently controls their actions and shapes their character like an inward fate—"England." It is this which gives hope in hopeless times, imparting

[1] If finally I were asked when this conception of empire began to take imaginative possession of the mind of a great statesman, I should point, perhaps arbitrarily, to Cromwell. And I should further point to Edmund Burke's great impeachment of Warren Hastings in 1788 as the period when, from being the possession of statesmen, it becomes the possession of the nation, shaping its counsels henceforth. For, if Burke is a reactionary in constitutional politics, in his impeachment of Hastings he is the prophet of a new era, the enunciator of an ideal which the later nineteenth century slowly endeavours to realize—an empire resting, not on violence, but on justice and freedom. That impeachment anticipates our present policy in India and in Egypt, just as Burke's speeches on the American Colonies anticipate the policy which underlies our treatment of Canada, Australia, New Zealand, and South Africa at the present day, a policy which has almost reversed an article of faith in the eighteenth century—that every colony must, in the long run, like ripe fruit, detach itself from the parent stem.

its immortal vigour to the statesman in his cabinet
and to the soldier in the field. A government or a
minister may seem to have the power arbitrarily
to provoke a war which involves the suffering and
deaths of thousands; but it is neither for government nor minister that the soldier falls. Lying
there in agony, sinking into darkness, he has in
himself the consciousness of this far greater thing,
this mysterious, deathless, onward-striving force,
call it God, call it Destiny—but name it England.
For England it is. It is for this that on the battlefield the soldier fights, in victory or in defeat.
This is the spirit-purpose which binds century to
century, making the yeoman who fought to establish an empire on the fields of France the comrades
in purpose of the mariners who founded Virginia,
of those adventurers to the East (themselves the
pioneers of the soldiers who, under Clive, Hastings,
Eyre Coote, Wellesley and Dalhousie, founded
our empire in India), or of those adventurers,
again, who settled in the vast loneliness of the
island continent of Australia.

To give all men within its bounds an English
mind—that has been the purpose of our empire
in the past. He who speaks of England's greatness
speaks of this. Her renown, her glory, it is this,
undying, imperishable, in the strictest sense of
that word. For if, in some cataclysm of Nature,
these islands and all that they embrace were over-
whelmed and sunk in sea-oblivion, if to-morrow's

sun rose upon an Englandless world, still this spirit and this purpose in other lands would fare on untouched amid the wreck.

To the German accusation cited in the opening lecture that in India England has made no new experiment in religion, it can be answered that more than any other conqueror of India she has permitted the genius of its race to continue its own developments, that religious propagandism has never formed part of her political creed. She has even, at stated intervals, checked the inopportune or intemperate zeal of missionaries of her own race. And how is it thinkable that an English Shah Jehan should ever arise to imperil by bigotry the continuance of the British Raj? At moments, indeed, this empire seems to resemble a vast temple, with the vaulted skies for its dome and the viewless bounds of this planet for its walls. And within that temple what prayers arise, in every accent, and what sound of hymns to every god that, down the long centuries, the human imagination has created or adored!

To give all men an English mind—that ideal has been our guiding star through all the phases of our empire.

> ". . . Se tu segui tua stella'
> Non puoi fallire a glorioso porto."[1]

[1] "If thou follow but thy star
Thou shalt not fail of a glorious haven."

And, until now, Dante's noble verse has been most strangely, most greatly realized by the English. Who shall affirm how long that ideal shall yet govern England's actions?

VI

WITH the twentieth century England has reached a stage in the career of empire when her policy, whatever it may have been in the past, becomes definitely a policy of peace, not war, of internal organization, not of outward expansion. England's task now, that is to say—if there were no other power than England—is the evolution, not of an exterior uniformity, but of an inner harmony, the organization of this empire that we already possess, the founding of an imperially representative government. New problems of every kind arising from within her own bounds are pressing for solution, in India, in Egypt, in Canada and in the Southern Seas. How is the central government of this vast and complex structure of empire ultimately to be organized? Who are to compose the Imperial Council or the Imperial Parliament? Upon what principle are its members to be elected, and from whom, and by whom? It seems as if the political genius of the nation or the empire were to be strained to create not only a new school of statesmen, but almost a new statesmanship. The problem of armaments, due to the transforma-

tion which the art of war is undergoing, is not less
pressing. If free communities, Canada, Australia,
New Zealand, South Africa, create their own
armies and build their own fleets, who is to have
the supreme command of those armies; in what
docks are those fleets to be built; by whom are
they to be manned; and what is to be the part of
each separate State or unit of government in their
control?   Is it conceivable, if those very principles
which have made England an empire are to persist
—the larger freedom, the higher justice—is it
conceivable that these organized countries, these
States already numbering some fifteen or sixteen
million inhabitants, will be content to supply the
means of peace and war and yet have no voice
whatever in the decision of peace and war? It is
absolutely inconceivable.   And, again, there is
that wider and still more intricate problem of
India. How and by what stretch of the imagination is that freedom and justice, in any conscious
or self-governing sense, to be extended to India?
And to that problem you can also add the like
problem in Egypt. These are merely the central
strands of a complex ganglion of questions which,
with every year and every decade, will become
more pressing.

Freedom a French thinker once defined as the
power to exercise the will in the pursuit of its
highest ends without fear. For this alone gives to
the mind that tranquillity, that "security," in the

strict sense of the word—immunity from cares—
necessary to free operations of the great faculties
of the mind. And it is this tranquillity, this security, that is now above all things necessary to
England. But it is just this tranquillity, this
security, which she cannot find. For whilst England may pray for peace in order to shape out these
problems in politics, there still beyond the North
Sea is the stern Watcher, unsleeping, unresting,
bound to her own fate, pursuing her own distant
goal undeviatingly, unfalteringly, weighing every
action of England, waiting for every sign of
England's weakness. It is here that Germany's
will to power comes into tragic conflict with
England's will to peace. Here is the element of
discord—it is not in England herself. What will
be the issue?

There the question lies, and it is a difficult
question—more difficult for a German than for an
Englishman. To talk about "friendly rivalry" is
no answer. I never can understand what meaning
that kind of talk has—"friendly rivalry," "generous emulation," and the image of racers on a race-
course. Even if such a thing were possible or
thinkable among nations—and there is no example
in history of any such "friendly rivalry," of any
such "generous emulation"—but even if it were
possible, what is to be the state of mind of a young
and ardent German at the present day who feels
within his nation very nearly an unlimited power,

and who sees only one great adversary, one great obstacle, between him and the realization of the world-ideal of his race? There are tens of thousands of such young Germans. What are you or I to think of them if they sit still and fold their hands—in "friendly rivalry," in "generous emulation" of England, a Power which is described to them by their leaders and thinkers as already tottering to its grave? What other spirit is to arise within them than the spirit which I have indicated in these lectures?

I have lived amongst Germans and know something of the temper of Germany's manhood and of her youth. I have read much in her history and in her literature. I have been impressed, as with the motion of tides and of great rivers, by the majesty of that movement by which, from the days of the Saxon and the Hohenstaufen Emperors, through centuries of feudal anarchy and disintegration made still more disintegrated by the convulsive forces of the fiercest religious strife, she has attained to her position to-day; and with the best will in the world I can see no issue to the present collision of ideals but a tragic issue. England, indeed, desires peace; England, indeed, it is certain, will never make war upon Germany; but how is the youth of Germany, the youth of that nation great in arts as in war, to acquiesce in the world-predominance of England? With what thoughts are they to read the history and the literature

of their country? If, from love of peace or dread
of war, Germany submits, it would seem as if her
great soldiers had fought in vain, as if the long
roll of her battles had passed like an empty sound,
as if the Great Elector and Frederick, Stein and
Scharnhorst and Bismarck had schemed in vain,
as if her thinkers had thought their thoughts and
her poets had dreamed their dreams not less in
vain. But if, on the other hand, Germany has
not declined from her ancient valour the issue is
certain, and a speedy issue.

It is war.

At the present stage of world-history it is, of
course, useless to seek a practical policy in arbitration. It would be a waste of words even to demonstrate the invalidity of this device. Nor would it
be more opportune to discuss the value of alliances
as a permanent means of securing the peace of
Europe. In a treaty with an enemy that treaty
is binding only so long as you can make your
enemy see gleam behind the parchment the point
of a sword; and the verdict of history upon alliances
is unmistakable and explicit. Whatever principle
may govern individual friendships, alliances between nations and States are governed by self-
interest only; they are valid only so long as mutual
fears or mutual desires persist in equal force. For
the friendship of nations is an empty name; peace
is at best a truce on the battlefield of Time; the
old myth or the old history of the struggle for

existence is behind us, but the struggle for power
—who is to assign bounds to its empire, or invent
an instrument for measuring its intensity?

In this country we seem to be gradually acquiring the dangerous habit of mind of trusting to
alliances rather than to our own strength. A great
nation trusts to itself mainly; only secondarily to
alliances, however intimate. For deep in the heart
of every nation lie ancient, strong resentments,
resentments that at a moment of crisis may flare
up into ancient strifes. War has often revealed
antagonisms between powers apparently friendly,
and sympathies between powers apparently hostile.
We speak much, for instance, of the Triple Entente; but of how long standing is our amity with
France, and upon what foundations does it rest?
Waterloo is not yet a century old, and Fashoda is
but yesterday; and some half a century ago, between these two terms, the ignoble terror of a
French invasion created the absurd Volunteer
System which a not less ignoble terror of Germany
has recently transformed into the still more absurd Territorial Force. And Russia? At the
present hour Germany seems in a state of dull
hostility towards Russia, England in a state of
very dull friendship with the same power. England, with her ancient dreams, her ancient traditions and ideals of the higher freedom, the larger
justice, summons the aid of Russia to help her to
govern, or misgovern, Persia! How can we hope

that such an alliance, so unnaturally framed, will last? Does it not contain within itself the very seeds of its own destruction? And along the northern shore of the Persian Gulf or on the Afghan frontier we have with our own hands laid a mine which might at any moment shatter the fabric to pieces. He who cannot take within his range a prostrate France and the alliance of Russia and Germany against England is not a student of politics, whatever else he may be.

There is possible perhaps for England another course than the arbitrament of war. Avoiding war and tacitly acquiescing in the rôle of submission, England may adopt a policy of concession to an enemy whom she dreads, and, one diplomatic defeat leading to another, she may gradually sink to a secondary place in the councils of Europe and of the world. In such a process there need be nothing that is crudely disgraceful, nothing to sting to the quick the honour of opportunist Cabinets or publicists. The concessions would be made at moderately wide intervals, and a people sunk of itself in torpor and indifference can easily be lulled by the ministerial management of words and events. Everyday life would go on as before; strikes would increase in number and the pillage of capital be accelerated; sloth would settle ever deeper on every class, and, as in the Byzantium of the thirteenth century, the vanity of a decrepit people would exhibit itself in complacent ostentation. Thus indeed the fate of England would resemble the fate of Venice in the sixteenth century, until some soldier, more cynical or more brutal in his ambition, would affix a term to her sham independence, as at Campo Formio Napoleon ended the sham independence of Venice.

But is the creative power which has shaped this ancient and famous empire really dead? Is it moribund, or sick at all, within us? Or is this momentary apathy and indifference a thing indeed momentary, that shall pass away?

Even now, even in 1913, when I consider England and this vast and complex fabric of empire which she has slowly reared, its colonies, its dependencies, the cosmic energy which everywhere seems to animate the mass in its united life and in its separate States or principalities, all such comparisons with decaying empires appear an irrelevance or a futility. Whatever be England's fate, it will not be the fate of Venice or Byzantium. And as a proof of the validity of this impression or this conviction I seem to discover everywhere stirrings as of a new life, to hear the tramp of armies fired by a newer chivalry than that of Creçy, and on the horizon to discern the outline of fleets manned by as heroic a resolve as were those of Nelson or Rodney.

England till now has known nothing of her danger. Democratic England has known nothing of war. The full enfranchisement of the English nation dates only from 1867 and 1885, and since 1867 what danger or what war upon a large scale has the enfranchised democracy experienced? But will not the democracy gradually understand that its own power and its own privileges depend upon the extent to which it takes upon itself not only the rights but the duties and responsibilities of those who have preceded it in the government of these islands; of the feudal barons who not merely fronted King John at Runnymede but led the charge on the fields of France from Crécy to Castillon; of the merchant-class who, in the sixteenth, seventeenth, and eighteenth centuries, rivalling in enterprise and daring the feudal leaders of an earlier time, outlined the wide bounds of our empire in the sunrise and in the sunset? . . .

[NOTE.—*The paragraph is unfinished. The lecturer must have intended to refer to the government and electorate which conducted and supported the war against Napoleon.*]

But in this is one's final hope: that the English nation and race as a whole shall gradually perceive that if the task of internal organization is ever to be carried out in that tranquillity and security of spirit which is necessary for all high tasks in politics, England must take upon herself the fulfilment of her destiny, depending upon herself alone for the realization of a destiny that is *her* destiny.

*   *   *   *   *

[NOTE.—*It was the author's intention to end the book with a fuller development of this theme of England and her destiny than was possible in the lecture. No notes for this intended close of the book exist except the following fragment.*]

And if the dire event of a war with Germany—if it *is* a dire event—should ever occur, there shall be seen upon this earth of ours a conflict which, beyond all others, will recall that description of the great Greek wars:

> "Heroes in battle with heroes,
> And above them the wrathful gods."

And one can imagine the ancient, mighty deity of all the Teutonic kindred, throned above the clouds, looking serenely down upon that conflict, upon his favourite children, the English and the Germans, locked in a death-struggle, smiling upon the heroism of that struggle, the heroism of the children of Odin the War-god!